Praise for *Rewiring Education*

"While others debate about if technology helps or hurts education, John Couch takes a more practical perspective. It is not about being for or against tech in the classroom, but rather about balance. *Rewiring Education* is an essential guide for every parent, teacher, and school administrator to better understand how to navigate (and indeed reinvent) education in the 21st century for the 21st century."

—**SIMON SINEK**, optimist and *The New York Times* bestselling author of *Start with Why* and *Leaders Eat Last*

"*Rewiring Education* bridges the gap between academic research and practice and proposes a pedagogy that integrates education, learning, and technology. Through personal anecdotes from a key industry insider, this book plants the seeds for a 'rewiring' movement that can unlock not just students' potential, but the potential of parents, teachers, and leaders at every level!"

—**DR. TODD ROSE**, author of *The End of Average* and head of the Laboratory for the Science of the Individual at Harvard University

"John D. Couch has been a pioneer in online learning. He is one of the first people to truly understand the power of technology in classrooms."

—**SAL KHAN**, founder of Khan Academy

"At a time of accelerating technological change, our education system must learn to adapt to the needs of the future. In *Rewiring Education*, John D. Couch explores important questions about education—not only how we teach but also what we teach—to open the debate about modernizing the school system."

—**HADI PARTOVI**, cofounder of Code.org

"John D. Couch is a true pioneer in using computers for education. His story and experience are important and should be known by all who care about kids and technology. Bravo!"

—**MARC PRENSKY**, author of *Education to Better Their World* and *Unleashing the Power of 21st-Century Kids*

"John Couch has written a most important book. Though his 'there at the beginning' account of Apple's prioritizing education is alone worth the price of admission, this is no history book. This is a call to arms, a tome to take seriously the brain's penchant for exploration, its negative reaction to current learning structures, its willingness to think different. Couch lucidly describes how the digital tools of the future can be exploited to take advantage of the brain's natural processing power. As he aptly declares, it's time to stop 'trying to repair and replace education and start rewiring it.' This tome belongs on your bookshelf or on your iPad."

—**DR. JOHN MEDINA**, *New York Times* bestselling author
of *Brain Rules* and molecular biologist

"Through *Rewiring Education*, John D. Couch has certainly earned his spot as the 'father of modern education.' His life and experiences portray true reflections on the need for change and how the world can achieve it. A deep and serious thought fantastically woven into a beautiful piece of literature that undoubtedly will be the 'scripture' for all educators in the days to come!"

—**RADHIKA LEE**, founder and director of the
Nairobi International School and author of *Rainbows in My Clouds*

"Our mission as educational leaders, compelled to advance our nation, must be to prepare our children for a complex world driven by exponential technological acceleration and fierce global competition. The extraordinary impact that results from inspiring every child's full potential can only be realized by thoughtfully and systematically incorporating instructional technology in every classroom across the United States. This incredible book by Apple Vice President John Couch is a must-read for every educator committed to transforming learning and every leader dedicated to creating a remarkable public education system."

—**DON HADDAD, ED.D**, superintendent of schools,
St. Vrain Valley School District

"John Couch is one of the most resilient human beings I know. Personally, professionally, his focus has always been on what is best for learning. His message never wavered. I love how he challenges his teams to think about how to leverage Apple's amazing ecosystem to improve the quality of life for classrooms everywhere. His clarity and advocacy in the power of connected multimedia personal devices, in conjunction with a challenge-based learning framework, changed how I taught on a daily basis. Steve Jobs talked about making a dent in the universe and John Couch definitely has been one of the best at making those dents. Since the day I met him, I could see why Steve Jobs was so inspired by him. This book, in my opinion, is only the beginning of the conversation John plans to extend to all of us to help reassess and rethink."

—**MARCO TORRES**, educator

Rewiring Education

Rewiring Education

How Technology Can Unlock

Every Student's Potential

John Couch
with Jason Towne

BenBella Books, Inc.
Dallas, TX

BenBella

BenBella Books, Inc.
10440 N. Central Expressway, Suite 800
Dallas, TX 75231
www.benbellabooks.com
Send feedback to feedback@benbellabooks.com

Printed in the United States of America
10 9 8 7 6 5 4 3 2 1

Library of Congress Cataloging-in-Publication Control Number: 2017055209
ISBN 9781944648435

Editing by Leah Wilson
Copyediting by James Fraleigh
Proofreading by Greg Teague and Cape Cod Compositors, Inc.
Indexing by Debra Bowman
Text design and composition by Silver Feather Design
Illustrations by weleniastudios
Author photo by Michael Soo
Cover design by Pete Garceau
Jacket design by Sarah Avinger
Printed by Lake Book Manufacturing

Distributed to the trade by Two Rivers Distribution, an Ingram brand
www.tworiversdistribution.com

Special discounts for bulk sales (minimum of 25 copies) are available.
Please contact Aida Herrera at aida@benbellabooks.com.

This book is dedicated to Steve Jobs, who challenged me to "think different" and helped me unlock my own latent potential.

To Steve and Janet Wozniak, for their continued encouragement throughout the years.

To Marco Torres, a teacher and visionary, who is an inspiration to everyone having the privilege of being in his company.

To my Apple team, the powerful and dedicated educators, programmers, and educational evangelists who have allowed me to stand on their shoulders.

To Dr. William Rankin, a unique college professor who was the first to implement mobile devices in his classroom, and whose ideas and insights are found throughout the pages of this book.

To Dr. Mallory Dwinal, a Rhodes Scholar with degrees from both Oxford and Harvard, who chose to forgo all of the luxurious things that her credentials could provide and opened a school to help the kids who needed it most.

To teachers everywhere, especially our Apple Distinguished Educators, who understand that all students are uniquely gifted.

To parents who know that children are capable of much more than our education system recognizes or allows them to achieve.

And last, but certainly not least, to my beloved children Kris, Tiffany, Jon, and Jordan, and my grandchildren, all of whom have provided me with decades of experience by being my own private research team.

Without any of you this book would not exist, and for all you've done I am grateful.

CONTENTS

FOREWORD

Having taught technology to fifth-grade students, I have witnessed firsthand the excitement and engagement it can bring to the learning process. But there aren't many people I know who truly understand this phenomenon more than my longtime friend and colleague, John Couch. I first met John back in 1978 just after he was hired as Apple's fifty-fourth employee by Steve Jobs. John was brought on as our first director of new products, and was soon promoted to be our vice president of software and lead the software team that created the graphical user interface.

Even back then John had a knack for simplifying and communicating complex ideas, and today there aren't many areas that need simplifying and fixing more than education. I can't remember a time when John wasn't passionate about education. I still remember the extraordinary stories he would tell of his time teaching at UC Berkeley and Cal State, or the decade he spent rebuilding a K–12 school in San Diego. It was no surprise to me at all then when, shortly after Steve Jobs rejoined Apple, John was brought back, this time as the company's first-ever vice president of education. Since that time he has been an integral part of Apple's ongoing efforts to transform education from passive traditions to active innovations.

This book might well be thought of as an inside look at all John's experiences—and, in a sense, Apple's—along the way. It takes the reader from Steve Jobs's passion for education, into the brains and minds of digital natives, and on to a new framework for learning that has the potential to make obsolete the consumption/ memorization model used today. Through personal anecdotes and the stories of real teachers, John explores new ways of learning and teaching. Last, he gives the reader a glimpse of future technologies that have the opportunity to usher in a truly personalized learning environment where every student can unlock their hidden potential and change the world. I believe that every parent, teacher, principal, politician, activist, innovator, and leader who is responsible for and/or passionate about teaching, learning, or training in any capacity will benefit greatly from reading this book.

—**STEVE WOZNIAK**
Cofounder, Apple Computer

INTRODUCTION

W hen I was growing up in the 1950s, the school curriculum focused entirely on memorization. The work we
did was not relevant, creative, collaborative, or challenging, but rather the simple consumption of information requir-
ing little more than short-term recall. Things were either black or
white; we either memorized the material or we didn't. And it was
understood that the seemingly never-ending series of standardized tests we were given would show how "smart" we were, in
the process judging us, labeling us, sorting us, and attempting to
forecast our future.

Today, when I speak, I often reference the inspiring Army slogan that once prompted us to "be all you can be!" The slogan of a great educational system should be the same—an education should make us feel that we can do anything we set our minds to and nothing can stop us. But for many of us sitting there at our desks, staring down at those omnipotent tests, that just wasn't the case. We were warned that these tests meant *everything* and would define us in the eyes of our teachers, families, friends, and future employers. Even then, watching many of my fellow students struggle with those tests, I knew there was something inherently wrong with the way things were. Scores on a test had led many of us to believe that perhaps we already *were* all that we could be.

I had always considered myself a good student. My parents read to me nightly, instilling a love of learning and discovery. I started reading young and was well prepared by the time I entered school. I absolutely loved those early grades, as they were more about discovering new things and just trying to learn how the world worked. Of course, we still had to learn the basics like arithmetic and spelling, but even those seemed interesting because my teachers made them fun and memorable. *If this was what school was like*, I thought, *then I was going to love it!* Then I entered middle school and everything changed.

Suddenly school felt a lot less like fun and a lot more like work. It was as if our natural creativity, which comes from simply being a child, was no longer valued or wanted. Whereas in elementary school we were these young, energetic "crazy ones," by the time we hit middle school it was expected that we would be over our craziness—that we would grow up and become better at fitting in. Explorations had been replaced by expectations, collaborating by competing, discovering by memorizing. And the praise we had always gotten for how unique we were now came only when we received good grades and high test scores.

If we did things differently in elementary school, it was considered creative, but when we did the same things in middle school it was considered coloring outside the lines. Learning felt no longer rewarding, but boring, and it began to show in my work. I knew that I needed to adapt, so I quickly learned to play what I refer to as the *education game*, one complete with points (GPA), scores (grades), levels (grade levels), winning (graduating), and losing (dropping out).

The character I became to play this education game was a *Memorizer*. Even though it was not my strength, it didn't require too much work, and it seemed to be the way to win the game. The more I memorized, the better my grades got, and the more I was respected and appreciated by adults. Unfortunately, I also noticed that some of my friends just weren't very good at playing this game. To me this made no sense, because I knew these were smart, creative kids who had thrived right along with me in elementary school. "What was happening?" I would wonder. The books and worksheets in middle school seemed pretty straightforward to me. "How can such smart kids be losing?" It seemed as if the education game was rigged against them.

THE WRONG GAME

When I graduated from high school, a classmate wrote in my yearbook, "Aristotle and Couch are now synonymous. Keep memorizing those problems!" It was meant as a compliment, but looking back, it really captures the main weakness of our current educational system: a focus on learning *what* to think, rather than *how* to think.

In middle and high school the rules of the education game were: take lecture notes, read the chapters, answer the questions, memorize the facts, and fill in the blanks on the tests. Then, based on our scores, we were rewarded with memberships in the National Honor Society, college acceptances and scholarships, and so on. By the time I graduated, I had the game all figured out—or so I thought.

I first attended college at the University of California, Riverside, where my memorizing evolved into cramming before exams. I made it through those so-called foundational courses in my freshman and sophomore years playing the same game I played in high school, and it seemed to be working. But then in my junior year, one of my physics classes suddenly changed the game. The final exam consisted of a single question: "Describe the motion of a spinning top in free space." It represented a daunting challenge, because the professor had never directly addressed the problem in any lecture, nor had the textbook covered it. I could hear sounds of bewilderment, frustration, and mounting panic all around the lecture hall as my classmates read the question. One student didn't even try to search his brain for an answer; he just dropped his exam—and textbook—into the trash and walked out. The class erupted in ovation. But I didn't clap, because I was still staring down at that question in stunned silence. I had no idea what to write. If an answer couldn't be memorized I was lost.

That exam question was life changing. I realized that trying to memorize my way through the rest of college, and through life, was not going to work. I realized education is not about memorizing, it's about learning how to think, and not a single book I had read had shown me how to do that. I had been playing the right game to succeed in the short term, but the rules I'd been playing by were totally useless for both this *new* game and for real life—which is the game school should have been preparing me for all along.

Later that school year I took a horticulture course that was equally as profound in shifting my understanding of learning—not to mention my career goals. I signed up for it solely because horticulture was one of the few departments that could afford an IBM computer and offered a course on computer programming. I was fascinated by the challenge of programming and the fact that there was never just one right answer. To pass this course, just like that physics exam with the spinning top, I couldn't just memorize my way through. What was required to succeed was *logic and visualization*—the type of thinking that leads to discovery. Some of my fellow students found the course difficult and frustrating, but I found it engaging and challenging. More important, that course was how I came to understand that for learning to be truly effective it must be based on the process of *problem solving.*

It was during that horticulture course that I fell in love with computers and their seemingly unlimited potential. I made up my mind that no matter what path my life eventually took, computers would play a significant role in it. However, since UC Riverside didn't offer an undergraduate degree in computer science, I needed to transfer to a different university. Despite the old African proverb, "Never test the depth of the water with both feet," I wanted to do just that with my newfound interest! I began searching for a college that offered an undergraduate degree in computer science, and found one at the Berkeley campus of the University of California, where I earned a bachelor's and a master's degree, and went on to enter their computer science PhD program.

Studying computer science excited me. Every time I was on a computer it made me feel empowered and in control, the way one might feel if they were suddenly freed from captivity. I felt that I could do anything—that I could once again "be all that I could be." It felt as if doors had magically opened, exposing an entire world that I hadn't previously known existed. I was Alice getting her first look at Wonderland.

In 1972, I accepted a job with Hewlett-Packard (HP), one of the biggest and most respected technology companies in the world. I felt like I was doing important work at the time, but several years later I received a phone call telling me about this small company led by a guy with a big vision—one that would change my life forever.

A MENTAL BICYCLE

"I want you to meet Steve Jobs," he said.

"Who?" I asked.

"He's the founder of Apple Computer."

It was a clear sunny day in the summer of 1978 when I received this call from my former supervisor at HP, Dr. Tom Whitney, who had recently become vice president of engineering at the up-and-coming tech start-up called Apple Computer. I had been a computer programmer and software manager at HP for five years, but had barely heard of Apple and wasn't quite sure why Tom was inviting me to his house in Los Altos to meet its founder.

"Okay," I told Tom. "I'll drop by." Of course, I had no idea as I hung up that phone that I would soon embark upon an extraordinary ride that would change my life and take me places I couldn't even imagine.

Meeting Steve Jobs for the first time was quite an experience. He was a bit eccentric and more passionate about his vision for the future than anyone I had ever met. He spoke of things that didn't exist yet as if they were foregone conclusions, and championed the so-called personal computer as the invention with the potential to make it all happen. Coming from the world of mainframe and minicomputers, I wasn't quite sure what to make of it all, but Steve sure did make it sound exciting!

During that first meeting, I came to understand that Steve's expertise was in hardware, and he was looking for someone with expertise in software, which is what led him to me. He shared a research study profiled in the magazine *Scientific American* that had explored which animal uses the least amount of energy to move over a given distance.[1] "The condor won," Steve said. "Humans didn't do as well. We're about a third of the way down the list!" Then the twist: The test was run again, but this time the human was placed on a bicycle. How efficient would a human be if they covered that same distance riding a bicycle? Steve grew excited telling me about it. "The man on the bicycle blew the condor away!" he said. "That's what the personal computer can be—a *mental* bicycle. It's the most remarkable tool in all of history."

Steve saw technology as an "amplifier for our intellect" in the same manner that a bicycle amplifies our physical ability. Not only would it take us faster and more efficiently to where we've already been, but it would also allow us to go beyond—to discover, create, and innovate like never before. As a graduate student in the 1960s, I had witnessed firsthand the social revolution that took place in the streets, at People's Park in Berkeley, and all around the Bay Area, but as Steve saw it, the true social revolution that would empower people would be technology.

Soon after that first meeting, Steve asked me to come down to Apple's office at Bandley One in Cupertino, where he offered me a job. I was a bit skeptical. At HP, we were building large computers that sold for $250,000, while Apple was building small personal computers that sold for $2,500, and Apple salaries were capped at $40,000, because Steve wanted people who shared his vision and didn't just see Apple as a financial opportunity. Even though that was only a fraction of what I was earning at HP, I had to admit that this new world of personal computers was intriguing.

I told Steve I'd consider the offer and went back to my office at HP, but it didn't take long for me to see just how persistent he could be. That Friday night I was at home with my family when the doorbell rang. I answered and saw Steve standing there with a box in his hand, smiling. "Hi John," he said. "Ready to change the world?"

Once inside, Steve opened his box and placed an Apple II on our kitchen table in front of my three-year-old son, Kristopher. He proceeded to show him how it worked and Kris instantly became immersed in it. "You know what, Kris," Steve told him. "If your dad comes to work for me, you can keep this." All I could do was laugh.

Steve and I continued to talk about the potential of technology, computers, and his far-reaching vision for the future. By the time he left, I too was starting to believe in its seemingly unlimited potential.

But it was watching Kris's behavior over the weekend as he "rode" the Apple II that had the biggest impact on me. My son was glued to the personal computer, so much so that he had stopped watching TV altogether and instead explored and created things that I didn't think a three-year-old could do. Most important, he was happily *learning* things, not because his teachers or parents required it, but because he wanted to. I could see Steve's vision of the future through the glow on my own son's face.

On Sunday, I told Kris not to get too attached to the computer because if I didn't take the job, it would have to be returned, and I was not sure I could accept the offer. "It's easy, Daddy," Kris told me. "Just say *yes*." The following week I left HP and became employee fifty-four at Apple, working directly with Steve Jobs.

Over the next several decades I was fortunate enough to have had a front-row seat as computer-based technology became a part of kids' lives all over the world. As for Kris, the technology bug never did leave him. By high school he was a virtual whiz who could already program, design, and write, and he produced a digital interactive presentation at the California High School History Fair that blew the judges away. He went on to graduate from the University of Pennsylvania in computer science, and his first job was on the team that designed eBay's website. In short, my son became the first of a new generation of "digital natives"—people for whom technology is viewed not as a tool, but as an environment for exploration.

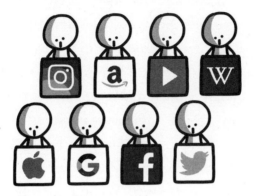

CHAPTER 1
REWIRING

If we teach today as we taught yesterday,
we rob our children of tomorrow.
—John Dewey

The term *digital native* was introduced in a paper written by entrepreneur and author Marc Prensky in 2001, and is generally applied to anyone born after 1979.[2] It describes those in the first generation to grow up in a digital world of personal computers, electronic games, tablets, and eventually cell phones. Today's high school students, for example, were born after the launch of Google and have never even known a world without the internet. They may have never used a library card catalog (or even a library card), choosing instead to rely on instantaneous web-based sources like search engines, Wikipedia, or YouTube for answers. New graduates were still elementary students when the original iPhone was introduced in 2007; today, four out of five seventh-graders have their own cell phones and are using a wealth of content and apps that are available to them 24/7.[3] The importance of this change is not just about the power of the devices, but about the platforms and ecosystems that bring the devices to life. Some refer to the digital natives growing up today as the "app generation."[4] While I often hear adults refer to modern technology as a "tool," digital natives see it as just a part of their environment, no different than how my generation perceived technologies like electricity. As a child, I didn't *use* electricity; electricity just *existed*.

Because of this, Prensky says, "digital natives think and process information in a fundamentally different way than their predecessors." Many cognitive neuroscientists disagree, arguing instead that *all* brains process information differently regardless of generation. However, there's no denying that the sheer amount of information that digital natives are exposed to via technology has greatly intensified both the number of changes occurring in the brain and the speed of which these changes are taking place. The truth is that today's kids have the ability to discover and learn more from a single mobile app than they ever could from any textbook ever written. "One of the biggest problems facing education," says Prensky, "is that teachers are speaking an outdated, pre-digital language and are struggling to teach a population that speaks almost entirely digital." The current educational system was designed to teach a very different set of children, in a very different world, with very different needs.

THE NEXT BIG THING

Today we live in a world of rapid technological innovation, where seemingly every day a new start-up comes out of nowhere with a new invention that changes things. Overflowing with creativity and empowered by the latest technologies, these visionaries from around the world have disrupted status quos, revised inefficient designs, upgraded outdated systems, and reshaped entire industries, except for one: education. There have been no revolutionary changes to our education system in the past century. Even where local successes at the school and classroom level show promise, nothing new ever seems to scale.

Take the story of one ambitious inventor who already had several successful inventions under his belt when he turned his attention to education reform. Like many of us, he found textbooks and lectures boring and believed that there had to be a better way to teach kids. He realized that our system was short-circuiting and needed rewiring. He went on to invent something that used the most advanced technology in existence and was unlike anything we had seen before. The inventor, and subsequently the media, loved it, declaring it something that would revolutionize education forever. Boring textbooks would now become a thing of the past. All students would now be able to learn equally, and our traditional classrooms, with their rowed desks, school bells, and a single teacher lecturing from the front of the class, would soon vanish forever. That invention was called an *educational film*, and was created by a guy named Thomas Edison in 1911.

Over a century later, it's evident that Edison's invention didn't work out too well, as not much has changed in our schools or classrooms. But how could that have happened? Edison had already succeeded at changing the world with his phonograph in 1877, the light bulb in 1879, and the motion picture camera in 1891, yet he couldn't make a dent in education. If one of the greatest inventors of all time couldn't overcome the obstacles blocking education reform, what hope do we have of overcoming them today? What's changed?

It may help to explore first what went wrong with Edison's educational-film idea. It turns out a group of intellectuals predicted the invention's failure, most notably a psychologist named John Dewey, who argued that it was more novel than practical, because he noted that kids learn best through hands-on, interactive learning, where they are actually *doing* things.[5] Dewey believed that sitting and watching content being taught to you on film was no different than sitting and watching content being taught to you in person. He argued that real learning was a social and interactive process that requires active participation, not passive observation.[6]

Since Edison's educational flop, hundreds of visionaries, innovators, and education reformers have followed his lead by introducing their own versions of the next big thing, and one by one, just like Edison's, each one failed. The reason? Dewey was right. Moving boring content from one medium to another doesn't make it any less boring, and doesn't improve learning. As much potential as technology has to improve education, unless it's used as a means to integrate proven methods of *learning*, and empower teachers to better deliver this learning, it is doomed to fail. To ensure the future of education that we want, at the scale that we want, technology and learning must be *integrated*. What's encouraging is that current and emerging innovations are indeed beginning to integrate the two, and the future looks bright, just like the light bulb—Edison's *real* game-changing invention. But change is needed to make that work.

Now, as Apple's long-time vice president of education, a father of four, and a grandfather of sixteen, I have been blessed with the experience of seeing technology and innovation empower extraordinary teaching and learning firsthand. I have visited many corners of the world and have seen for myself some of the best and the worst educational systems. I've now been involved in education and technology for over five decades and have witnessed governments, districts, schools, teachers, entrepreneurs, and parents try various means to improve our education system. These changes have been offered in two broad ways: *repairing* parts of the system and *replacing* the entire system. Unfortunately, neither is likely to bring forth the type of change that's needed.

REPAIR AND REPLACE

The most common method used to improve education is to apply tactical, short-term fixes, such as Edison's educational films. They typically attempt to tackle one specific aspect of education—in this case the ability to make learning more fun and interesting. Today, educational videos called *explainers* are successfully doing exactly that. They take what are often boring lessons, transform them into documentary-like cartoons, and suddenly they're more interesting. But as interesting and informative as these videos are, they have been around for decades (remember *Schoolhouse Rock?*) and still have not made a major dent in how we deliver education throughout our schools.

I like to look at the specific pieces of education that need to be fixed as being what those in the software world would call "bugs." Computer bugs are flawed bits of code that cause the system to behave in unintended ways. To fix these bugs, engineers could start over and rewrite the whole program, but that would not be very efficient. Instead, they develop "patches," minor enhancements designed to quickly fix the problem at hand.

This is what happens in education, too. It's much easier to fix an educational bug with a quick patch—more testing, lowering class sizes, updating a curriculum to a fancy new framework—than to fix the system itself. Make no mistake, though: quickly fixing a bug is not necessarily bad. If you have a nosebleed, then a tissue would certainly come in handy to contain it, even if it doesn't fix the core problem making it bleed. So while I'm by no means saying that patching education is useless, it is limited—and often these repair efforts only provide a small fix that proves hard to scale up. Patches are too small and do too little to fix fundamental problems with education, especially those facing digital natives.

The second most common way that reform is typically introduced goes to the other extreme, suggesting that our entire public education system is broken and that only *replacing* it with something else completely, such as private, charter, or online schools, is the answer. In the technology world this would equal throwing the entire computer system in the trash and buying a new one—ignoring, of course, that it too will likely be out of date in a few years. In fact, there's a very popular idea, known as Moore's Law, which has shown that the rate of technological change has become so rapid that the processing speed of new computers doubles every eighteen months! It's not just processing speed either—the truth is, all technological change is happening at an exponential rate. How many times have you finally gotten that new smartphone, tablet, or other wireless gadget, only to have it supplanted a year later by an all-new model? Trying to keep up with the latest hardware is difficult—and expensive.

The same is true in education. Almost every year I hear another education reformer suggesting that we need to toss out our entire educational system and start anew. Ideas like private, charter, and online schools have been suggested recently as better ways to rethink the entire system. While these models have shown some success, the truth is they are often just as static as the systems they are trying to replace and, just like technology, are complex, expensive, and offer no guarantee that they would actually be *better*, rather than just *different*.

Unfortunately, neither making individual repairs to our system, nor replacing it with another similarly static system, are viable options, primarily because our world is constantly changing. Society changes, leadership changes, technology changes, families change, children change, and so do our expectations. It's "Moore's Law of Education" in a way: the accelerating pace of technological development leads every new generation of students to find itself immersed in a different world than their parents', along with their specific needs. Our only real solution is to learn, adapt, and change along with them.

REWIRING EDUCATION

Like a computer, education needs a system prepared to meet the needs of its current generation—in our case, digital natives. It also needs leaders with the ability and agility to ensure the system is designed, developed, and implemented to keep pace with change. So far that has not been the case. Much of our educational system is outdated and disconnected, perpetually struggling to meet the needs of the users (both students *and* teachers) who depend on it. Repairing (patching) and replacing (starting over) education is not the answer. What's really needed is *rewiring*—upgrading our educational operating system so that it better connects students, teachers, parents, and society, and so that our schools can foster creativity and innovative thinking. Only by rewiring the system can we adapt to changes *as they occur*, without the fear of proposed updates short-circuiting it all: moving away from passive models of education and toward active models of learning.

Rewiring education means meeting the biggest challenges we face in education today: how to use learning research and current technology to personalize learning experiences in ways that better meet the needs of today's students. It asks us to think differently about how we motivate, train, develop, measure, and evaluate our children and the extraordinary people who teach them. And it means understanding and unlocking the unlimited potential for children to learn and succeed.

I tend to be a bit hard on our educational system, and the reason is because I love it—at least I love the potential of it. The truth is that I think our educational system is among the best in the world for *some* kids, but I want it to become the best for *all* kids. Unfortunately, that same education game that I had to play as a child persists today, and that's what's driving many of the inequalities. Everything can become better, even the things we love. Yet interestingly, the flaws in the system that prevent us from improving didn't get there by accident, but were put there by design.

CHAPTER 2
DESIGN

Our students have changed radically.
Today's students are no longer the people
our educational system was designed to teach.
—Marc Prensky

Picture for a moment a classroom full of students happily learning new concepts in unique and interesting ways. The teacher here does very little lecturing, knowing that every student in the class learns differently and at a different speed. So instead of lecturing to a standard curriculum, this teacher has each student working on the same topic, but in different areas and at a different pace. Essentially, the teacher has personalized the learning for each student.

When I describe this scenario to many people in education circles, I usually get a slight chuckle, followed by an immediate dismissal. "That's ideal," they say, "but it's wishful thinking." One person called it a *utopian dream* that, he said, "could never be done on any large scale in America." Another simply shook her head and smiled, saying, "That's how it should be, but it would take a *miracle* to make it actually happen in this country."

What they did not know at the time, however, is that the scenario that I'm describing has actually already happened—all across America. It's exactly how teachers in nearly all of the classic, one-room schoolhouses in the early 1800s taught.[7] It wasn't the future I was describing; it was the *past*.

So, what happened? How did we lose that level of customized learning? While historians can point to dozens of reasons (e.g., population growth), the change can actually be traced back to an event that took place on March 20, 1856, in Philadelphia, Pennsylvania. This event would later prove to be the beginning of the end of customized learning and teaching for the next hundred years. It was not a war, depression, or assassination that changed the course of educational history, but rather the single idea of a man named Fred.

ONE BEST WAY

As a child, Frederick Taylor was not unlike many other children growing up at the time. He was born into a Quaker family; his father was a wealthy attorney, and his mother a feisty abolitionist. After being homeschooled by his mother, Taylor studied abroad, then attended Phillips Exeter Academy, an elite private school in Exeter, New Hampshire. He earned an undergraduate degree from the Stevens Institute of Technology, then worked as a mechanical engineer, developing a knack for getting things done quickly and efficiently. In fact, he proved to be so much more efficient in his work that he began to question why others could not be just as efficient as he was. Factory workers, he noted, were often intentionally doing less work than he knew they were capable of, and he despised it—he believed it hurt his employers' bottom line. In an effort to change things, Taylor extensively studied efficiency and productivity, putting his findings into his 1911 book *The Principles of Scientific Management*.

With their zeal for maximizing efficiency and productivity, Taylor's ideas swept the country, making his book one of the most influential management guides of all time. His concepts transformed all types of businesses and organizations by eliminating "waste" (and skilled workers) in many industries by breaking jobs into small, individual tasks nearly anyone could do. This change saved employers a lot of money, as they would not have to pay for skilled professionals. It also meant that they needed a great number of *unskilled* workers to replace those skilled professionals. Managers didn't need or want their workers to be very smart; to maximize productivity and output, according to "Taylorism," it was management's job to be smart, and the worker's job to do the tasks exactly as assigned.

It was at this point that work in the United States began being equated with *quantity* rather than *quality*. It was no longer about how good you were, but how fast you were. Speed was much easier to quantify and used to hold people accountable. Energized by the theories of scientific management, industry focused not on customization or creativity, which bogged down efficiency, but on *standardization*. This led people like Henry Ford, the founder of Ford Motor Company, to standardize his car manufacturing for mass production by adding assembly lines and low-skilled workers. In the world of standardization, the organization always came before the individual.

Many workers back then had big ideas and dreamed of being entrepreneurs like Andrew Carnegie and J. P. Morgan. They wanted the American Dream that had been promised to them. Being just another cog in a well-oiled system was not what they had in mind. Which meant if industry was going to continue to grow rapidly, they needed to produce the cheap, mindless labor required to fill all those unskilled jobs. And the best way to do that, thought John D. Rockefeller—the world's richest man and arguably the most well-known entrepreneur of the time—was to start early. That meant changing education to better prepare kids for the workforce.

If there's one thing Rockefeller understood as head of the Standard Oil Trust oil production and refining monopoly, it was how to make more money. Getting to this peak in the business world was hard, and Rockefeller was in no hurry to let it slip away, which is what led him to become interested in grade school education. For their companies to continue to grow and succeed, Rockefeller and his kind desperately needed a large supply of low-skilled but hard-working employees. Luckily for these business leaders, the ideas behind scientific management were proving quite popular across industries—including education.

In 1912, just one year after the publication of Taylor's book, the world of education was met with its own paradigm-changing piece of literature: an influential essay rethinking the purpose of school-based education as no longer one that would prepare kids for life, but instead for the kind of labor needed at the time. The essay was essentially a how-to guide for ensuring enough low-skilled workers remained available, saying at one point:

> We shall not try to make these people or any of their children into philosophers or men of learning or of science. We are not to raise up from among them authors, orators, poets, or men of letters. We shall not search for embryo great artists, painters, musicians . . . nor lawyers, doctors, preachers, politicians, statesmen, of whom we have ample supply . . . The task that we set before ourselves is very simple as well as very beautiful . . . we will organize our children into a little community and teach them to do in a perfect way the things their fathers and mothers are doing in an imperfect way.[8]

The essay was drafted and published by a group that called itself the General Education Board, founded and funded by none other than Rockefeller himself. The "Taylorists," as those who agreed with Taylor's ideas came to be known, fervently made the case that the purpose of formal schooling should be to provide a "standard education for an average student," essentially preparing them for blue collar jobs within the Industrial Revolution, rather than encouraging higher-level thinking or fostering creativity. Interestingly enough, as we'll see later, debate over what schools should be preparing students for continues today.

A later follower of Taylorism was the psychologist Edward Thorndike, who became a huge proponent of standardization in schools, believing they should separate kids based on their abilities so that they could be "appointed" to their appropriate place in life. Only by doing this, he argued, could school funding and resources be used effectively and efficiently. Thorndike and his ilk did not believe that all students were equal, rather that some were simply superior, and it was they the focus should be on. Those less capable, in his view, didn't deserve the same opportunities. They were basically, and should be treated as, *factory workers*.

For Taylor, Thorndike, and their followers, there was always "one best way" to do *anything*; any deviation would result in lost productivity and greater waste. And one best way meant standardization. Suddenly, teachers began being trained differently. They were now held accountable for how many students were able to pass specific tests, rather than how much progress they made. There were right and wrong ways to teach and you either taught the right way or you were fired. Students were taught the exact same material, in the exact same way, at the exact same speed, regardless of their capabilities as individuals. If the efficiency model said that people on average *could* learn math in a certain way, at a certain age, then that's exactly what *should* happen. It was the inherent inequalities born from ideas like this that redefined our schools during the later phases of the U.S. Industrial Revolution, and kicked off a focus on standardization throughout our education system that persists even today.[9] In 1915, a day after his fifty-ninth birthday, Frederick Taylor died of pneumonia. While widely regarded as a legend in business, he became a pariah in education, especially to those of us trying to improve individual learning experiences.

As I think through the history of education in the United States, I marvel at the parallels between it and my own family's educational history. My great-grandfather, born in 1867, had a third-grade education. My grandfather, born in 1902, had an eighth-grade education. My mother, born in 1926, had a high school education. And I, born in 1947, was the first in my family to graduate from college, even earning a graduate degree in computer science. I was later followed into higher education by all four of my children. This leaves me optimistic that we're at least moving in the right direction—just too slowly and with a number of challenges to still overcome.

DEBUGGING THE SYSTEM

It has now been over a century since the Industrial Revolution. Politicians, school administrators, and others argue every year for the need to increase educational rigor and give all kids equal opportunities to learn, yet the standardized model still dominates. K–12 teachers are expected to ensure that every student in their classrooms is "at grade level" no matter their talents, preferences, strengths, weaknesses, or backgrounds. The students who do end up succeeding tend to be memorizers who have learned to play the same education game I did decades ago.

So how do we change it? It's certainly not going to be easy, but I believe we have to start from the inside and then move out. In other words, before utilizing technology, let's make sure we understand psychology. Before we put our faith in systems, reforms, or patches, we must put it in our kids. We must believe and understand that *all* of them can learn and succeed. Like the

Taylorists of the past, many teachers, knowingly or not, continue to write off kids who struggle as those who "just don't get it," due to the ever-present pressure they feel from endless assessments and accountability measures. This attitude toward struggling students isn't about apathy, but survival—a kind of defense mechanism that allows them to feel sympathy, but still justify the fact that they must keep moving—or risk the whole class falling behind! This highlights one of the most damaging flaws of the standardized system: it uses artificial timelines that allow the pace of the class to drive learning, rather than the pace of the individuals within it. But classes are not individuals and cannot be taught, nor can they learn. Only the individual students within them have the capabilities to learn and succeed. Successfully rewiring education requires us to focus first and foremost on students as individuals, then on learning, teaching, and the proper use of technology.

We cannot change systems; we can only change people, who must then work together to change systems. Our most powerful weapon, though, is our ability to change ourselves. We must start by asking ourselves if we truly believe that *every* child has the potential to learn and succeed. Because, deep down, if we don't believe that, there's no point in pursuing reform and no amount of technology will help. If there's one thing I've learned by working with Steve Jobs and other extraordinary leaders, it is that transformation always starts from within and works its way out. Once we believe in kids, in our hearts, they will start believing in themselves, and we'll be on our way to helping them unlock the potential they never knew they had!

CHAPTER 3

POTENTIAL

*Education should no longer be mostly
imparting knowledge, but must take a new path,
seeking the release of human potential.*
—Maria Montessori

T odd was a classic underachiever with a long history of behavioral and motivational problems that reportedly had caused him to struggle throughout grade school. After multiple detentions and suspensions in high school, he dropped out with a 0.9 GPA. As if school wasn't difficult enough for Todd, he had the added responsibility of taking care of his pregnant girlfriend and their forthcoming child. He ended up taking a job paying less than $5 an hour and subsidizing it with welfare checks.

Those who knew him said that he was a good kid, that he was smart, and that he had a lot of potential. Clearly something had gone wrong at some point along the way. "I was a square peg in the round hole of our school system," he reflected years later.

I often hear people describe kids who struggle through school, get bad grades, or drop out with words like *lazy* or *dumb*. Those who are more sympathetic might instead cast the blame for kids like Todd on his parents' lack of attention, poor teachers, or perhaps a lack of funding for intervention programs. "But what if kids like Todd are *our* fault?" I sometimes ask during the speeches I give to educators and school administrators around the country.

A lot of confused faces stare back at me. "How could he be *our* fault?" they think. "After all, we don't even know Todd!"

That is true. They don't know Todd. But after hearing just a few cherry-picked facts about his life, they, like many of us, would have jumped to certain assumptions about him, or about his family or teachers or available resources. But I see the real problem not being whatever we attribute his failings to, but rather our tendency to make assumptions about him at all. This is the primary failing in our current system of learning and teaching: we limit students' potential based on what we *assume* they are capable of, rather than making it possible for them to show us.

STARTING FROM WITHIN

Successfully rewiring education begins not with technology, but with psychology. There are persistent misunderstandings about kids' potential to succeed and we must take these into account before trying to help. What happened with Todd is that we often fall victim to a psychological phenomenon in which our minds have a way of oversimplifying complex things we don't understand. This phenomenon, which psychologists call the *fallacy of the single cause*, causes us to look for one easy-to-understand answer to a problem that is actually quite complex. Often this answer is the first thing that comes to our minds as the "cause" of a problem after we're first made aware of it, but before we know all the surrounding circumstances. We may not even know that we don't know all of these circumstances; it's as though the further we are from something, the simpler it seems to us. For instance, we may have read a news article about Todd and suddenly consider ourselves fully informed, not realizing that articles and news clips on TV also carry this bias.

The fallacy of the single cause is related to another phenomenon called *cognitive bias*, which is when we make judgments about people or things based on our *own* personal experiences or circumstances. For example, if we dropped out of high school because our teachers were not very good, we might hear Todd's story and, without realizing that it's *ourselves* that we're thinking about, subconsciously blame poor teaching for his woes as well. A social worker may blame socioeconomic factors, because they witness them on a daily basis; a psychologist may blame mental or emotional issues; and a successful person who found a way to succeed in school in spite of the odds may blame Todd himself for just not trying hard enough. And they all think they know this through experience!

The reality is that none, a few, or all of these may be the actual cause of a person's failure. Cognitive bias is dangerous if we're not aware of it, because personal beliefs can cause flawed laws to be written, bad rules to be implemented, and potential opportunities to be withheld for the wrong reasons. Just as dangerous is *confirmation bias*, which occurs once we've made up our minds on what we believe to be the cause, and then subconsciously proceed to do everything in our power to *prove* ourselves right, rather than to learn the real reasons. As it turns out, if we look hard enough for proof that our theories are right—even if they're not—we can almost always find a way to justify them.

Understanding that thoughts about a student's success are happening within our own minds, consciously choosing to reject them, and admitting to ourselves that there is more to the student's success, or lack thereof, than we may know are the first steps in making real change. Recognizing our biases is at the heart of my idea of rewiring education by starting from within.

ROSE-COLORED GLASSES

Not long after Todd dropped out of high school, he was fortunate enough to find mentors who saw and accepted him as the square peg that he was. They encouraged him to follow his passions, ignore the past, and not to listen to any of the naysayers. They convinced him that he could do *anything* he wanted, regardless of where he was currently or where he'd been in the past. It took time, but eventually Todd began to believe it, and once he became fully convinced that he really *could* do anything he wanted, things began to change. Within just a few years he had put his past behind him and entered college—a goal he'd previously thought of as an impossible dream.

Today Todd is known as Dr. Todd Rose, an esteemed Harvard professor and the faculty director of the Mind, Brain, and Education program at the Harvard Graduate School of Education. He's also the president and cofounder of the Center for Individual Opportunity, and is renowned for his groundbreaking work in education. He has an undergraduate degree in psychology, and both his master's and doctorate are from Harvard. At one point Todd was listed in *The Improper Bostonian* magazine as "one of the smartest people in the Boston area"—quite a feat considering it's the home of both Harvard and MIT.[10] He has also authored two critically acclaimed books, *Square Peg: My Story and What It Means for Raising Innovators, Visionaries, & Out-of-the-Box Thinkers* and *The End of Average: How We Succeed in a World That Values Sameness*, and is working on his third, *Dark Horses*. In them, he shares his groundbreaking research into what is known as the science of the individual. "We are all square pegs to some degree," he explains, "spending most of our youth trying to figure out how to fit into the round holes given to us by society." Just as no two snowflakes are exactly alike, each person is unique, an individual, and this individuality matters. Only by understanding people as individuals—by rejecting use of the average as the primary yardstick against which we measure ourselves and others—can we learn to really make a difference in their lives.

"Society compels each of us to conform to certain narrow expectations in order to succeed in school, our career, and in life," Dr. Rose says. "We all strive to be like everyone else—or, even more accurately, we all strive to be like everyone else, only better." A lot of people had written Todd off early as a child, consciously or not. I see his story as a reminder that, when we see a struggling child and realize our brain's initial instinct is to label them as an underachiever (or worse), perhaps we should place that instinct in check and instead try seeing them through Rose-colored glasses.[11]

RELATIVITY MATTERS

Once we accept that we are all plagued by cognitive fallacies and driven by confirmation bias, we can begin working toward identifying them in ourselves and pushing back when necessary. Dr. Rose's work on individuality shows scientifically what common sense already tells us: everyone is different. Not just physically, but also in how we learn things and the speed at which we learn them. We're also different in the way we view and define things. Sure, a dictionary can give us a general definition of a word, but many words will always mean different things to different people. For example, if I asked you what it means to be "successful," you might equate that to financial success, whereas I might equate it to the impact someone has had in a particular field, regardless of financial gain.

The same is true when it comes to determining the perceived success of students. There is no one answer to the question of what makes a student successful. People could point to a variety of things including GPA, test scores, passing/failing, learning progress, and so forth. In other words, success is a *relative* concept, rather than an *absolute* one, just as is someone's *potential* to succeed.

This is why I believe that *every* student has the potential to succeed. I don't necessarily mean that every student has the potential to memorize an entire textbook in order to pass a standardized test; I mean that every student has the potential to succeed in their own *individual* way. Relativity matters. Whether or not someone is "living up" to his or her potential to succeed is simply a matter of point of view.

Consider two children, a boy and a girl, both considered equally intelligent. Our job is to determine whether each is operating at their full potential. The boy gets straight As in school and does little else but study. When he does take time for an extracurricular activity, he plays soccer, which he doesn't care for and finds not very competitive. Nonetheless, he is physically fit and clearly *capable* of doing better in soccer if he really wanted to. Meanwhile, the girl gets a lot of Bs and Cs, but her despairing parents know that she is *capable* of getting straight As. As proof, they point to her amazing violin playing, on which she spends the majority of her spare time practicing. During music class, she's able to memorize both written and audible music, yet in most other classes she struggles. Her parents assume she's just not trying hard enough in her academic classes.

In this scenario, is the boy maximizing his potential? Is the girl? Both? Neither? If we ask the boy's English teacher we will get one answer, while his soccer coach would give another. If we ask the girl's math teacher he would insist that she's not, but her music teacher would disagree.

The point of this exercise is that we cannot determine whether or not a child is living up to their potential without first answering the question: potential to do *what*? Let's say, for example, that we're only discussing academic potential in terms of grades. What if a student gets straight As in English, but Bs or Cs in math? Does this mean that they aren't operating at full potential in math? Digging deeper into their math skills, we find that they are mastering fractions and decimals, but struggle in geometry. We also learn that they only struggle with certain *types* of geometry problems, and only when they're taught in a certain way. For a parent or teacher to try to figure this out for just one child takes a lot of effort. It's much easier for us to just look at that B or C grade and conclude that the child is struggling in a certain subject. Student success and failure are most often not a problem of potential, but one of perception. And since perception is relative, like success and potential, our *expectations* for any given child's success must be relative as well, as they can directly affect the realization of that potential.

LAYERED EXPECTATIONS

Teachers often find themselves in quite a dilemma: choosing between keeping a steady pace to ensure that *most* of their students remain adequately challenged, or slowing the pace of their teaching down to ensure that *all* of their students have mastered the material. While teaching at a set pace and reaching thirty students may be ideal, we know that just isn't feasible. As we'll see later, adaptive technology can play a very important role in solving this dilemma, but technology is only as good as the software that runs it—software designed by humans. To know how best to write this software, we must first get a better understanding of ourselves, of what's important and what's not, and of what our expectations are, and should be, for our students.

Many experts argue that we should have equally high expectations for *all* students, pointing to *grade-level standards* as the most effective means of ensuring this. "If we don't maintain equally high standards for every student," the argument goes, "then we are hurting kids by not believing in their true potential." I hear this argument from school activists, policymakers, administrators, and well-meaning politicians. Many others argue in favor of keeping things "realistic," with proponents pointing to *progress indicators* as the most valuable tools for setting expectations. "If we don't keep expectations realistic," they say, "we'll be setting kids up for failure." It's often teachers, especially those who teach at-risk students, who make the case for realism.

I believe that both contain elements of truth. Yes, we should have high expectations for *all* students, and we often underestimate the potential of a child to grasp concepts once they have been taught to them in ways to which they can better relate. I find that most of the time it's not that they can't learn something, it's just that they can't learn it the way it's being taught. My fear is that by setting low goals in an attempt to be realistic, we could be hindering our students' chances at doing great things. To me, if a child isn't understanding something that's being taught to them, it isn't the child's responsibility to figure it out; it's up to the teacher or parent to figure out how to teach it differently so that they do understand.

On the other hand, our expectations for student learning should not be based on any set-in-stone standards, the likes of which kids are all expected to achieve *at the same point in time*; rather, our expectations should be relative to a child's *current* abilities. Not that I don't expect a student to be able to divide mixed fractions; just maybe not in the third week of the fourth month of fifth grade! If the student is in fifth grade and knows little more than addition and subtraction, my immediate expectations for him would be to learn multiplication and division, while a *future* expectation would be to also master fractions. High expectations should not be synonymous with immediate expectations; instead, expectations should be *layered*, both immediate and future.

Standardized tests don't capture a child's progress. What they do is measure content knowledge against *other* students in similar grades. As methods for judging the success or learning potential of any individual student, they are ineffective. As a friend once put it, "The only thing standardized tests measure accurately is how well students can prepare for standardized tests!" Unfortunately, because teachers are commonly judged (and sometimes *paid*) according to the results of the standardized test scores of the majority of their students, they find themselves believing in one thing (equality), but feeling as though they have to do another (keep it moving), which dampens their expectations for many of their students as well as for themselves.

It's dilemmas like this that commonly undermine the potential for every student to achieve at high levels. Yes, I know that, despite all of my talk of psychological phenomena and layered expectations, there are still a lot of skeptical people out there who deep down don't believe that the sky is the limit for every child. In their minds, there are clear limits to what can and can't be accomplished by people, and they believe that many just seem to be *born* to achieve better than others, which touches on the age-old *nature versus nurture* debate that has raged on for decades.

NATURE VERSUS NURTURE

In the late nineteenth century, a diminutive statistician by the name of Sir Francis Galton became intrigued by a theory that a person's ability to learn things was genetic and must be inherited.

Galton is perhaps most recognizable as the father of *eugenics*, a misguided set of ideas and practices that aimed to "improve the genetic quality of the human population" and that inspired Adolf Hitler to write the infamous *Mein Kampf* in 1925, which ultimately led to his attempted extermination of the Jewish people (among others) and a world war. Nonetheless, eugenics wasn't Galton's only big idea, as he is also responsible for the phrase "nature versus nurture," a concept he covered in depth in his 1869 book, *Hereditary Genius*, on his ideas of genius and greatness.

The nature-versus-nurture debate has dominated educational theory for decades. Proponents of the theory believed that nature is largely responsible for our intelligence and abilities, and that because of this we can only learn and achieve so much. They argued that we're all born a certain way—some naturally smart, others naturally athletic, others with no natural abilities at all. In other words, our potential is all in our genes. On the other side of the debate were those who believed that nurture, not nature, is what matters. They argued that we are born with clean slates and it's our environment as we grow and develop that counts most.[12] This debate continues to some degree today in educational circles, but recent findings indicate that the answer is not so simple as either nature or nurture.

Research now suggests that, while of course we do inherit genes from our parents, including ones that contribute to intelligence, our environment (i.e., the things we experience) is key to how those genes are expressed, and even if they are expressed at all. One of the most promising new fields of scientific study is called *epigenetics*. Epigenetics demonstrates that the expression of our genes (i.e., nature) is not static, but dynamic. It can and does change over time. Our environment (i.e., nurture) affects and collaborates with our genes, forcing them to adapt. So our biological genes work together with environmental factors in what amounts to not nature *or* nurture, but nature *and* nurture. It's the collaboration between the two that really matters.

Neurologists are now studying one part of epigenetics, called *interactionism*, that focuses on how our genes dynamically interact with our intelligence. The work done on interactionism so far suggests that the main benefit of being born with "good" genes, neurologically speaking, is that it may allow for more rapid learning of certain things in certain ways. Nonetheless, it's now clear that things like what we do, how we do it, and who we hang around can actually change our physical brain and hereditary intelligence level. As David Shenk, author of the book *The Genius in All of Us*, puts it, "People actually affect their own genome's behavior with their actions." So, in a way both sides of the debate are right, but also wrong.[13]

Alas, I can hear the pushback now: "What about students that are either born with a limited intellectual ability, or have failed to acquire this ability? Should we honestly expect a higher level of success from them? Maybe the Taylorists are right! We do need blue collar workers! After all, someone has to clean our toilets and run our factory lines, right? Why kid ourselves to think everyone is equal, when we all know they're not?" These are the type of things I hear when people are attempting to justify the idea that not everyone is created equal and, because of this, we should not focus much on equality in education at all. "Perhaps," they feel, "our expectations for the potential of some kids should just be tempered, rather than layered." I strongly disagree. I believe we should prepare every child to be *extraordinary*, which means making opportunities available to them to be so, and that begins with a quality education. Life will then intercede, driven either by the decisions they make or circumstances outside their control, and will fill many of its more ordinary roles along the way.

I think that those who make such arguments about equality are confusing being equal with being unique. Uniqueness is related to individuality (i.e., who we are), whereas equality is related to opportunity (i.e., what we're capable of doing). Again, as Dr. Rose's research points out, we are all born unique and remain that way for the rest of our lives, and that's a good thing. We are not, however, all born equal, but luckily that's something that can, and should, be changed. As we'll see, technology, when used correctly, can be one of the biggest educational equalizers the world has ever seen. But it was critical for us first to gain a better understanding of potential and of our own biases, so that we can move on to the next phase of rewiring education—motivating kids to actually realize that potential.

CHAPTER 4

MOTIVATION

Education is not the filling of a pail,
but the lighting of a fire.
—WILLIAM BUTLER YEATS

The most important component to achieving success is motivation. I've argued for years that if a person is motivated enough to succeed, we would have a very difficult time stopping them from doing so. The same is true in education. If a student wants to learn about something badly enough, a bad parent, teacher, and school combined could not stop them from learning it. This is why kids can memorize the words to entire songs, but can't seem to remember a math formula they were taught five minutes ago. It's the reason they can use critical thinking skills to solve complex problems posed by a character in a video game, but can't tap into that same skill to figure out what they're supposed to do next in a math word problem. And it's the reason why many boys with dreams of becoming professional athletes find the time to play basketball for hours each day, but not to do their algebra homework.[14] The reason for all of this is that *motivation matters most*. If kids are struggling to learn something, most often it's not that they *can't* learn it, but that we just haven't convinced them that it's *worth* learning.

SWEET SPOTS

When discussing the importance of motivation, I like to relay the story of my daughter, Tiffany. Tiffany's older brother, Kris, excelled academically, but she struggled in school and we were concerned that she might have some sort of learning disability. No matter how certain topics were taught to her, either at school or by us at home, she always seemed to need extra time to understand things. However, she always did well in any topic related to arts and crafts. By the time she entered middle school, the person we hired to tutor her, Lillian Leaberman, had quickly recognized Tiffany's innate artistic talents and that she was a visual-kinetic learner. She helped Tiffany build a model house in a Middle Ages town and craft Elizabethan-era dolls by hand. Tiffany always had the biggest smile on her face whenever she was creating things, but I had never connected the passion she had for artistic pursuits with her average performance in the more traditional academic areas.

Tiffany went on to enter college as a psychology major. By then she had learned to channel her focus and did well. But during her sophomore year, a sorority sister came across some of Tiffany's artwork and was blown away. "This is magnificent! You have a natural talent for art and design, why in the world are you wasting your time in psych?" she asked. The words hit Tiffany hard and before long she had left her major and decided to follow her passion for art, transferring to Otis-Parsons Design College and changing her major to fashion. After that there would be no more struggling, because she was doing what she loved to do and, as with any properly motivated student, success was not far behind.

I remember not long after Tiffany had started at Otis, she said to me, while flashing that same smile she had as a child as she crafted her dolls, "I spent fourteen years pushing the education ball up the hill, until I realized my natural gifts and my passion, and now I can finally chase the educational ball down the hill!" She went on to receive a special honor, winning the Thimble Award, one of the most coveted awards the school had to offer.

As a parent, what I've learned from these experiences with Tiffany is that parents and teachers all too often think that if a child is not succeeding academically, there must be something wrong with them. It turned out that the only learning disability Tiffany ever had in school was a lack of motivation. Once she recognized and began taking advantage of the "sweet spot" between her passions and talents, she was able to begin realizing her true potential.

My experiences with Tiffany cemented my belief that teaching children should be primarily about helping them discover their own natural genius, interests, and passions. I've found over the years that almost every child has what I call their *sweet spot*.

Sometimes, but not always, this is easy to find, because we tend to be passionate about the things we're good at—which is likely why we're good at them in the first place. However, there are plenty of kids (and adults for that matter) who have no idea what it is they're passionate about, or who may be good at something they are not passionate about, or who may be passionate about something they just aren't very good at. I believe a primary goal of both educators and parents should be to help kids discover their own individual sweet spots by figuring out what they're good at and what they *want* to learn, and then tying it in with the things they *need* to learn. Of course, I realize that's always easier said than done.

STUDENT MOTIVATION

One of the hard truths about learning to motivate people, much less a classroom full of students, is that teachers are not being taught how to motivate their students and are left on their own to figure it out over time. With all the talk about what the best standards and teaching methods might be, very few are effective unless students are engaged and motivated enough to want to learn what's being taught. On the contrary, highly motivated students can (and likely will) learn just about anything, even in the face of subpar teaching and minimal resources.

I believe motivation is a *prerequisite* for effective learning. You likely won't find many educators who would disagree with this, yet motivation is rarely taught or even talked about in teacher training programs. Most schools of education have no formal focus on it, and the ones that cover it at all typically do so as little more than a single lesson tucked within an educational psychology elective.

The question is: *Why?* If the importance of motivation is such common knowledge, why isn't it talked about more often?

One of the reasons we don't hear a lot about student motivation, and the main reason science and schools of education ignore it, is because it's notoriously difficult to measure *quantitatively*. We cannot tell by reading a test score or looking at a GPA how motivated a child is. We can *ask* them, but that moves away from the neatly packaged quantitative analyses that scholars and practitioners rely on. Things like polls and surveys are more in the *qualitative* realm that's often brushed off as anecdotal evidence rather than hard empirical evidence. Even qualitatively, if we give students questionnaires or poll them, there's a significant chance that they will provide the answer that they think we (adults) want to hear rather than tell us how they really feel. Nonetheless, even without volumes of quantitative data on how student motivation affects their performance, there are lots of theories on motivation, each with their own research and studies on what works and what doesn't.[15]

SELF-DETERMINATION

By far the most studied and accepted among the motivational theories is self-determination theory (SDT). This theory is primarily concerned with understanding people's inherent needs and growth. Edward Deci and Richard Ryan, the codevelopers of the theory,[16] are two of the world's most cited modern-day psychologists. Their academic papers on SDT are considered to be the most authoritative work ever done on the topic of motivation. For the purposes of rewiring education, there are a few key takeaways from SDT that I feel will help us better understand student motivation.

Self-determination theory looks at the choices people make and *why* they make them. More specifically, it looks at whether or not these choices are made with or without the person being influenced by someone or something else. For example, if a student chooses to spend the majority of their free time studying math problems, is it because they need to get an A on a test and raise their GPA, or because they just really, really love math? If it's the latter, then SDT refers to it as *intrinsic motivation*, whereas if it's the former, according to SDT, it would be a form of *extrinsic motivation*.

Of course, there may also be some crossover between intrinsic and extrinsic motivation as well, and SDT takes that into account by looking at the degree to which one outweighs the other. In terms of education, the easiest way to think about the difference between the two types of motivation is that *intrinsic* motivation is when a student is motivated primarily by something *within*, such as in the earlier examples of kids playing video games or basketball. *Extrinsic* motivation is when a student is motivated primarily by external factors, such as test scores, grades, awards, or someone like their teacher, parents, or a coach.

Educational proponents of SDT argue that what we want is for kids to be intrinsically motivated to learn academics. Volumes of research suggest that when people are intrinsically motivated to learn, the learning lasts longer, understanding of the topics is improved, and recall is better and longer. Getting kids to be intrinsically motivated to learn is the holy grail of academic success, but also happens to be one of the most difficult things to do.[17]

Certain types of extrinsic motivation, however, have been shown to offer pretty good short-term positive results. The irony is that while nearly every educator, researcher, administrator, and public official with any knowledge about learning will agree that intrinsic motivation is preferred, our entire educational system has been designed and implemented to rely on extrinsic motivators like grades and test scores. Extrinsic motivation is good for the short term and is how our system has been designed; intrinsic motivation is better for the long term and is how our system *should* be designed. We're already able to rewire our system to better align with the research behind intrinsic motivation, but until we're willing to do so, we will have a difficult time nurturing an inherent love of learning in many of our students. When it comes to rewiring education, it's important to be able to differentiate between the two, because, as we'll see, technology has the power to use both types of motivation effectively.

THE ART OF MOTIVATION

There is indeed a lot of science and psychology behind motivation, but it can be just as much an art. Like most complex things—and despite what Taylorists might believe—there is no "one right way" to boost motivation. All variables must be taken in context. What motivates me today might not motivate me tomorrow. One type of game may motivate you while other types do not. Remember, we're talking about something related to the mind, and minds have a funny way of changing depending on circumstances. That being said, over the years I've accumulated many helpful suggestions and tips, either from my own experiences or others'. Here are a few of the most important.

Student Choice

The first has to do with the idea of choice. Giving kids choices in how they learn things can go a long way toward making it more engaging.[18] The more engaged kids become, the more motivated they become to remain engaged. This does not necessarily mean they are motivated by the topic we're teaching them, but rather by how we're teaching it. Making learning fun, engaging, and relevant are keys to making nearly every learning experience better.

Along the same lines as student choice is student pressure. What used to be more characteristic of angry parents on the sidelines at a youth sports game has now crossed over into the world of education. Parents everywhere are putting more and more pressure on their kids to succeed. Pressure leads to stress, and stress leads to all sorts of negative things. As a parent, I certainly understand that we all want what's best for our children, and I'm not suggesting that we shouldn't "push them" to become even better. What I'm suggesting is that if we do choose to *encourage* them, at least let them have a say in what it is they're being encouraged to do. Ensuring that they are emotionally and mentally invested in their goals is the key to helping kids achieve them.

I recall recently hearing one parent say to their fourth-grader, "Either aim to be the best in the world at everything you do or don't bother doing it." I felt the same frustration the fourth-grader no doubt did, and I'm sure we both had the same question: "Why?"

Not long after watching the poor kid get admonished for not being "the best," I broached the topic with a close colleague of mine. "Do parents really believe that making their kid sacrifice the best parts of their childhood is worth it?" I asked. "Shouldn't the child have some say in the matter?"

She turned the tables on me and asked what I would do if it were my own son, and he was the one saying he wanted to be the best and wanted to be pushed. "Well, in that situation then I would probably do it, because it's his choice," I replied.

"And what if he changed his mind once the hard work started and wanted to quit?" she asked. "Would you let him? Would you explain that greatness laughs at the very idea of quitting, or would you let him move on, knowing that the opportunity to succeed in that endeavor can vanish over time?"

I didn't know what to say. It's a dilemma many parents regularly struggle with, and one each of us has to solve for ourselves. Should we sacrifice the present in the *hope* of a better tomorrow? Should a child?

One thing I know is that in order to decide, we must first really *understand* the child. If we know deep down that what they're asking for is *their* dream, and not our dream *for* them, then I might resist the urge to let them quit. I find that it's often better to let them explore, discover, play, and just be a kid while they still can. Only when it's clear what *really* motivates them will the magic happen, with or without us.

Realistic: To Be or Not?

The second helpful tip has to do with realism. "Keep it real," the saying goes. I've always been a big believer that anything is possible. Rarely will you ever catch me using the word "impossible" as I've seen way too much happen over the course of my life that I would have thought was impossible. People deemed pretty much everything Steve Jobs said he was going to do to be impossible at the time he first mentioned it. It's because of my own experiences at Apple learning to make the impossible possible that I have come to dislike the whole idea of "being realistic." This is especially true when it comes to talking with kids who have big dreams. Many of these dreams are unlikely to happen, but that doesn't mean they won't happen.

When my coauthor, Jason, speaks to inner-city high school students, he does so in a somewhat unorthodox way. For example, he often starts the conversation by asking the kids, "Who here has dreams of becoming a professional athlete?" Nearly all of the boys' hands shoot into the air. "Well, I believe you'll make it and I'm going to help you get there," he tells them. He's then met with several looks of bewilderment, not just from the students wondering how he's going to pull off such a feat, but also from the school's administrators wondering why he's talking about professional sports instead of not dropping out of school!

The odds of making it as a professional athlete are less than 1 percent and everybody in that room knows it. So why would Jason say that to them? "How are you going to do that?" he's asked.

"Well," he replies, "we all know it's going to be hard for you, so let's walk through the steps. Let's use NBA basketball as the example. What would improve your chances of making it into the NBA the most?" he asks. Inevitably the idea of playing for a major college basketball team like Duke, Kansas, or Kentucky comes up, and that's when Jason makes his move. "That's right," he agrees. "Your chances of making it into the NBA go up dramatically if you play basketball for any one of those teams. So, for starters, let's work on getting you into one of those schools. I'll make you a deal: you guys work on getting your skills up to par on the court, and I'll help you get into one of those schools."

Suddenly the students all smile and get excited as hope flashes across their faces.

What just happened here? Jason just got an entire group of students, most of whom were on the verge of dropping out of high school, to get excited about the possibility of attending a major university. The kids know it will be difficult, but they also know it's not impossible. Since the guy just told them that he dropped out of high school himself and still ended up attending Harvard, they are pretty confident that there must be a chance for them to succeed as well. The first step, though, is succeeding in school—right now!

Most of the well-meaning adults these kids deal with hit them with hard doses of "reality," reminding them of how slim the odds are that they will succeed, and suggesting they drop their wild dreams and focus instead on a more realistic Plan B. But all the kids hear when adults say that to them is, "That's hard to do. It's too hard for you. I don't believe in you. You're not special enough to be in that 1 percent." Do not let this happen to your kids. Don't be a dream killer by spreading harmful ideas about what you consider to be more realistic; instead, find a way to tie whatever it is they think they want with whatever it is you think they need.

Always being "realistic" destroys our ability to think differently and stay creative. It confines us to the limited expectations of the present, or of the person telling us to "be realistic." After all, what we perceive to be realistic may be quite different from what even our own neighbors, coworkers, and friends do. I experienced this firsthand at HP. In the early days, we were constantly told to be realistic, that it would be impossible to compete with IBM, since they "owned the computer business" and you should "never attack a well-built fortress." Luckily, we didn't listen.

Failing, to Learn

The third helpful tip has to do with the ideas of failing and deliberate practice. This is particularly interesting, because most of us are not typically big on doing things where we see ourselves as failing. We tend to focus on doing the things that we do well and stay away from the things we don't. This means that unless a parent, teacher, or coach relays to a child that failing is encouraged and expected, they will likely see it as bad. This is what ultimately prevents most of us from reaching the top level at anything. We've been taught that if we fail, we've *failed*, and that's the end, rather than seeing it as a step on the road, or as a necessary part of the learning process. We learn not in *spite* of our failures, but *because* of them.

Apple has always been known for innovation. But one of the things Steve Jobs expected of us, even in those very early days, goes counter to almost everything you may have heard about Apple: he expected us to ignore the past, push the envelope of the present, and *create* the future. Short-term failures were encouraged as long as they happened in the process of aiming for long-term success. In fact, if we didn't have any short-term failures, it meant that we weren't innovating enough. We were expected to push boundaries and that only happens through trial (try) and error (fail). That mandate to fail our way to success is what ultimately made us stand apart from our competitors.

I believe that we should not just accept but encourage a pattern of intelligent failing by kids. In fact, research on expertise describes the process of *deliberate practice*, in which experts in a variety of fields live in a constant state of failing because that's how they train and get better.

I have argued for decades that everyone is uniquely gifted and that there is genius buried within all of us, whether it's related to math, science, art, writing, problem solving, playing, or something else. In those early years, I had only anecdotal evidence, but in the early 1990s I discovered the quantitative research studies and experiments done by K. Anders Ericsson, a psychologist and expert on expertise, and others that showed convincing evidence that a person can reach almost any level of expertise in a chosen subject— as long as they're approaching the subject in a particular *way*.

As it turns out, I was not the only one inspired by Ericsson's findings. Before long our country's growing fascination with higher performance had led to several bestselling books on the topic, including *Talent Is Overrated: What Really Separates World-Class Performers from Everybody Else* by Geoff Colvin; *Outliers: The Story of Success* by Malcolm Gladwell; and *The Talent Code: Greatness Isn't Born. It's Grown. Here's How.* by Daniel Coyle. In 2016, Ericsson finally coauthored his own book on the topic, *Peak: Secrets from the New Science of Expertise*. Each of these books tackles expertise from different angles, but even as they became popularized via headline-grabbing words like *talent*, *success*, and *expertise*, what they were fundamentally about was *learning*, and it was my goal to understand how that fit in with K–12 kids who might not need to become world-class performers, but just *better* performers.

What Ericsson's studies on expert performance concluded was that what we often refer to as *natural* talent is actually the result of practice. While this may sound blatantly obvious, the trick is that it isn't regular practice that's required, but rather deliberate practice (a concept widely popularized by Gladwell's book, *Outliers*). Deliberate practice is not the same as "drill and kill" practices or memorization exercises, which are both extremely limited in their usefulness. What's needed, Ericsson explains, are repeated attempts to reach beyond one's current level, in which something specific is learned from each failure and the difficulty is increased each time—kind of like what happens in video games, where there are multiple levels of challenges. Doing this for a long enough period of time (around ten thousand hours, according to research) offers the highest chance of reaching expert level in a chosen field, especially if it's tied to something at which the person is naturally gifted.[19]

Ericsson's groundbreaking work led all of the aforementioned authors to provide anecdotes from Mozart to Michael Jordan showing individuals who were not born with genius or gifted-ness, but who acquired it through a learned, deliberate process. What this implies in the context of student motivation and learning potential is that we should presume that all students have the ability to learn *anything*, and that the best way to increase focus is to improve the *ways* in which we teach them. And along the way there will be a lot of important failing going on.

The Grit Factor

My final motivational tip is for parents, teachers, and leaders to keep in mind that while failing is *required* for learning, the perseverance needed to accept and deal with those failings is just as important. As Winston Churchill said, "Continuous effort, not strength or intelligence, is the key to unlocking our potential." Whether we call it persistence, perseverance, resiliency, or grit, I consider ensuring that students have it, and finding ways of increasing it, as being vital pieces of rewiring education.

Angela Duckworth is a psychologist and professor at the University of Pennsylvania who is best known for her book *Grit: The Power and Passion of Perseverance*. Rather than focus on the relationship between intelligence and achievement, Duckworth's work examines how other, noncognitive differences in individuals might be better predictors of success. This led her to "grit."

Grit, as defined by Duckworth, is one's ability to persevere in the pursuit of long-term goals. In her research, Duckworth studied GPAs among college undergraduates at Ivy League schools, retention rates in some very tough classes at West Point Military Academy, and rankings at the National Spelling Bee. She confirmed that IQ and other standardized tests are indeed poor predictors of long-term success. What came the closest to predicting who succeeded and who did not was grit. Duckworth concluded, "Achievement in difficult goals entails not only talent, but the sustained and focused application of talent over time." What this means is that perseverance is a better predictor of success than any single-score test.

Duckworth's findings ask: Is grit innate, an inherited trait that we are born with, or could it be taught? While there has been some pushback on the topic, Duckworth is in the process of showing that it can indeed be taught, and several major studies are attempting to prove it.[20] That's great news, but I feel a lot more attention must be paid to the role of motivation.

Just as genes are expressed differently depending on their environment, character traits like grit are situational, dependent on context. In the case of grit, I see it as depending on how motivated a person is to achieve a particular goal and, in the spirit of self-determination theory, *why* they want to achieve it.

MOTIVATION TO LEARN

In education, we often hear about the achievement gap, a constant problem in which there are large disparities in academic performance between groups of students, mostly by race and socioeconomic status. What we don't hear about is the *motivation gap*—the gap that I believe exists between kids who are highly motivated to learn and those who are not. Unfortunately, there are a lot of students who are not intrinsically motivated, but that doesn't mean they can't achieve and succeed at high levels. It just means that we must find other ways of motivating them. Todd Rose became motivated because mentors believed in him until he began believing in himself. Tiffany became motivated when others recognized her talents and openly questioned why she wasn't taking advantage of them. Others are self-motivated, like my youngest son, Jordan, and it's their own burning initiative that takes on learning journeys—sometimes about the strangest things.

In 2001, for example, when Jordan was in tenth grade, he came home from school one day and said, "I have to do a science project." I asked what he was thinking about doing and he replied, "I've been reading about deformed frogs that were first found in 1995 and are now reported in thirty-two states. I'm really interested in what's causing the deformity." I pointed out that his teacher wouldn't have the answer, and there was probably not a book in the library or even a scientific journal article about it, but he was undeterred.

Jordan went off to do some research and found out that there were three theories about the possible cause: ultraviolet light connected with ozone layer depletion, agricultural pesticides washing into ponds where the frogs live, or a parasite found in the affected frogs. He said he was going to email the professor who wrote the article he had originally read about the parasite. "I'm going to see where I can get hold of one of these parasites. I'm going to take the DNA of the parasite and compare it with the known protein involved in limb generation." He knew about a website where you could submit a DNA sequence and receive information about whether the sequence existed, whether it was patented or published, and what it was homologous to.

Before long, Jordan heard back from the professor, Dr. Stanley Sessions, at Horwick College in New York state, who seemed delighted that a high school student was interested enough in his work to track him down. He promised, "I can show you a pond outside Portland, Oregon, that contains snails infested with parasites." The professor agreed to meet Jordan in Oregon, and not long after, Jordan left, toting his digital camera and iBook, ready to capture everything he could to help him on his science project.

My son learned that the parasites that cause the deformities were hosted in snails. Jordan and the professor packed up some of the snails in dry ice and flew back to New York. Under an electron microscope (at midnight!), they were able to see the parasites exit the snails. The professor showed him how to extract and amplify the parasite's DNA, and Jordan submitted the DNA sequence to the website. The report came back confirming that the parasite was 98 percent homologous with a known protein involved in limb generation. He wrote up the findings, describing the situation as "similar to terrorists entering the cockpit of an airplane, removing the pilot, and taking the plane in a different direction."

Jordan's work won the high school science fair award. A few weeks later, Stanford's Doug Brutlag, a Distinguished Bio-informatics Expert, got in touch to ask him if he'd like to spend his summer at Stanford, continuing his research. "No," Jordan told him matter-of-factly, "I play basketball in the summer!" Not long after, I was on a plane reading *USA Today* and noticed an article reporting that Yale University has been awarded a $2.6 million grant to study deformed frogs, but Jordan, aged sixteen, had already published the results of his research—on the *internet*.

I like to share this story when I speak as a way to highlight the role that initiative plays in potential. Jordan was incredibly self-motivated, and all I needed to do was stay out of his way and support his built-in initiative whenever he asked. Unfortunately, not every child has Jordan's level of initiative, but every child can be motivated to learn in one way or another. While the good news is that we know what works when it comes to motivating kids in general, it's our job to get to know what motivates them individually.

In terms of motivation, rewiring education means helping kids discover their sweet spots, encouraging and nurturing an intrinsic love of learning and self-determination, and believing that they can be as successful as they want to be, doing whatever it is *they* want to do. This will lead to more self-confidence, grit, initiative, and, ultimately, better *learning*.

CHAPTER 5

LEARNING

Learning is not attained by chance,
it must be sought for with ardor and diligence.
—ABIGAIL ADAMS

n Professor Karen Brennan's "T-553: Learning, Teaching, and Technology" class at the Harvard Graduate School of Education, the assignment on the first day asks her hundred-plus students to each submit a one-sentence description of what they believe the purpose of education should be. It's not uncommon for them to look around at one another, a bit perplexed about what may come across as a rather simplistic assignment, especially for graduate students who have already dedicated their lives to the topic!

The students are given a few minutes to type up their one-sentence purposes and then submit them electronically. Once all the submissions are in, a teacher's assistant collates them, removes the students' names, and then broadcasts the sentences onto the smartboard.

Several answers always come up in one form or another, such as, "To prepare students for jobs," "To prepare students for college," "To teach critical thinking skills," "To develop good citizens," and "To help students learn to think independently." But dozens of new, and sometimes creative, answers turn up in every class.

"What do you notice?" Brennan asks them. "They're all different," her students note. It turns out that every one of her students has within them a different idea of what the purpose of education should be. She has never once gotten two sentences exactly alike.

The point of Professor Brennan's exercise isn't to get her students to come to a unanimous decision on what the purpose of education should be, but to make them aware that not only does everyone not have the same understanding as they do, but that *no one* does! It's an eye-opening experience for her students as it forces them to examine their own biases, assumptions, and preconceived ideas, on the very first day of class. We have a tendency to believe that everyone else thinks like we do, but in reality, that's hardly ever the case, even among people who share the same goals. If these hundred budding education experts in the same class, at the same school, can't even agree on what education should do, it's no wonder that it's been so difficult to improve it for millions of students across the country.

While it's true that most people can't agree on the purpose of education, what most of them *do* agree on is that at the very center of it is *learning*. Whether a student has been properly *educated* is an opinion and cannot be proven, but whether or not they have *learned* is a fact that can be assessed. Once we become more aware of our own biases, believe that *every* student has the potential to succeed, and begin motivating them to *want* to learn, the next step in rewiring education is to shift our focus away from the broader concept of education, and toward a narrower definition of learning.

WHAT IT MEANS TO LEARN

Along with asking her students for their own views on the purpose of education, Professor Brennan also asks them on day one to write one-sentence personal definitions for *learning* (and *teaching* as well, but we'll get to that later!). Just as with *education*, she always receives a lot of variety about how they define learning, so I think it's important to clarify right up front what it is we mean by the word. If we look up the meaning in the dictionary we get a vast array of definitions, including "to acquire *knowledge* of something," "to become *informed* or acquainted with something," and "to *memorize* something."

What we most often mean by "to acquire knowledge of something" is to learn *about* something. In this definition, the noun "knowledge" refers to information. So, in other words, this definition is referring to us getting information about something. To me that's not learning, that's researching. While there may be some useful short-term learning going on in terms of information, there is no indication that any real learning is taking place.

The second definition, "to become informed or acquainted with something," is basically the same thing, referring more to a temporary retrieval of information, rather than any longer-term usage.

Last, "to memorize something" is just about the worst definition of learning I can think of. Just because we can define something doesn't mean we actually know anything about it—it just means we've memorized the definition. The difference is something like this: memorizing is the storage of static information inside of our brains, whereas learning is understanding what that information means and how best to use it in various contexts. Memorization isn't learning; if anything, it's only a small component of a complex learning process.

To simplify things, I like to think of there being three different things going on when it comes to learning: *retrieving* (being able to find facts), *memorizing* (being able to remember facts), and *understanding* (being able to use facts). Today, technology has now made retrieving facts extremely easy while making memorizing them nearly useless, leaving only understanding—the most critical of these elements. Learning is not about the facts themselves, but about understanding what to *make* of them and what to *do* with them. Facts are merely puzzle pieces, not the puzzle itself. If you're new to puzzles, then you could either spend your time memorizing the pieces of your current puzzle, or understanding how puzzles work so that you can become good at solving all of them.

Whenever I speak and get to the part about my thoughts on education versus learning, I share the chart at the top of the next page that compares the two and sums them up quite nicely.

	EDUCATION	LEARNING
OVERALL PARADIGM	Delivery	Discovery
SOCIAL STRUCTURE	Hierarchy	Community
CONTEXT	Classroom	World
ENVIRONMENT	Simulated	Real
CONTENT	Fixed	Open
ASSIGNMENTS	Recipes	Frameworks
ACTIVITIES	Consumption and Repetition	Construction and Creation
INFRASTRUCTURE	Administrative Focus	Student Focus
ASSESSMENT	Teacher-driven	Community-driven
PROCESS	Standardized	Personalized
MOTIVATION	Extrinsic	Intrinsic
EXPECTATION	Grades and Certification	Skills and Experience

Chart courtesy of Dr. William Rankin

Early in his career as a schoolteacher, Ben Orlin asked his tenth-grade trigonometry students, "What's the sine of $\pi/2$?" They responded in unison, "One!" accompanied by calls, "We learned that last year." It was only later in the year that Orlin would discover, "They did not really know what 'sine' even meant. They'd simply memorized a fact." To Orlin's students, "math wasn't a process of logical discovery and thoughtful exploration, but a collection of non-rhyming lyrics to the lamest sing-along ever." He found that his students never had any trouble figuring out what to do to succeed in math, as he explains: "Memorize the necessary facts ten minutes before class, and then forget them ten minutes after class." I don't think anyone can honestly argue that Orlin's students had *learned* trigonometry, just because they knew the answer to a math fact.

Orlin's story reminds me of my own experiences playing the education game. We hadn't needed any relevant understanding of topics, we just memorized what needed to be memorized and promptly forgot it. That was until that darn spinning-top question!

Once we accept that real learning means the understanding (or comprehension) of things within various contexts, we quickly realize that much of what we're doing in schools is just wrong. Rewiring education ultimately means changing the way we teach the things we want today's students to learn. It should no longer be about distributing content and memorizing meaningless facts, but about teaching kids to combine new understandings of these facts with critical and creative thinking skills that ultimately lead them to discover, understand, and create new things. Maybe it's just me, but this sure does sound like it might be a pretty good one-liner for the purpose of education.

Brain Rules

I find Professor Brennan's classroom word experiment fascinating because it so clearly represents a prominent theme throughout all of education: everyone is different. Students, teachers, parents, administrators, researchers, and everyone in between all harbor unique backgrounds, strengths and weaknesses, biases, motivations, goals, dreams, points of view, learning capabilities, and even *brains*.

John Medina, author of the book *Brain Rules*, has spent decades studying the brain and has a gift for simplifying complex concepts.

His work revolves around what he refers to as the "Twelve Principles of Surviving and Thriving at Work, Home, and School." While Medina explains in lay terms a great deal of things that affect the brain (i.e., sleep, stress, survival, etc.), he also spends a lot of time covering the brain's wiring itself. "What we learn throughout our lives changes what our brain physically looks like," Medina says, explaining how all sources of input (sight, sound, touch, smell) work to create new connections between our neurons—which in turn leads to new memories.[21]

"Everybody's brain is wired differently, even in the presence of the same event," Medina says. Just as Todd Rose's science of the individual has shown us how different we all are from social-science and psychological perspectives, Medina's work backs that up by showing us how physically different our brains are as well. "Each person's brain develops at different paces and in different patterns, with no two people having the same brain roadmap," Medina says. All of our brains are simply "wired" differently, which in turn means we learn certain things differently, in different ways, and at different speeds. This is the biggest problem with relying on standardization in education—there simply are no *standard* (*average*) learners for us to teach.

So, what does all of this mean in terms of learning? For me it's even more proof of just how unique we all are, and not just from one another. We're also unique in terms of ourselves, over time. I may technically still be the same guy I was forty years ago, but how much of who I was then is who I am today? With a physically different brain that changes over time, passions and motivations that also evolve, and millions of experiences that have occurred across that span, I think it's safe to say I'm a totally different person. It's not just me, either. As kids grow, the changes they endure dwarf those of adults. It's not just hormones that are changing; their brains are, too! And when brains change, the way they process things like learning changes as well.

The Relatability Factor

In 2014, a study done at the Stanford University School of Medicine looked at how children of different ages learned math problems. What they discovered was that small children learn quite differently than older children, teens, and adults. "As the children aged," the researchers found, "they gradually switched from solving problems by counting on their fingers to pulling facts from memory."

The results of the study, published in the journal *Nature Neuroscience*, showed that small children use their brains' hippocampus and prefrontal cortices (which together are responsible for short-term or "working" memory) almost exclusively when trying to solve problems, while teens and adults rely more on the area of the brain called the neocortex (which is responsible for long-term memory).[22]

In other words, small children have fewer long-term memories to rely on, so their brains instead try to solve problems with whatever resources they have access to, such as using their fingers to count. As kids get older and acquire more memories, they have a wider selection of memories to pull from, and that is where things get interesting.

When we think of a child's memory in terms of learning, we tend to refer to the recalling of facts, but recalling facts has much more to do with memorization than actual learning. In learning our memory goes into overdrive, not just recalling facts but *experiences* as well. Many of our experiences stay locked away in our long-term memory, ready to use when called upon. As we get older we're constantly, whether consciously or not, learning new things through our experiences, and we're also better able to make connections between these experiences. So when we run across something new our brain goes into overdrive trying to find some memory to latch on to that will help put that new information or idea into perspective. We are always searching for these connections, and the more memories we have access to, the easier it is for us to relate to new problems and grasp new ideas.

This *relatability factor* is our way of trying to make sense of the world, but also helps explain why some people have an easier time learning certain things than other people: they have more memories related to a particular new piece of information or idea to cling to. It turns out that learning may have more to do with our preexisting experiences than it does with how smart we are.

Educators can learn a lot from these findings. For example, perhaps we should put less effort toward trying to force memorized content and more effort toward trying to find ways of tying new information to older information already stored in students' long-term memories. The most effective ways of teaching an unknown concept to a student is by relating it to a known one, and this is why learning *must* become more personalized.

Personalized Learning

Personalizing our learning means tailoring it to each student. It's teaching and learning for students as *individuals* rather than using the one-size-fits-all methods that spawned from the Taylorists and have refused to die ever since.

Just to be clear, personalized learning does not mean that there must be a 1:1 teacher/student ratio, that every student must have different textbooks and tests, that every student should learn in isolation, or that homeschooling is better than sending kids to a physical school. While solutions like these can be more effective for some kids, they are not very realistic solutions when dealing with education as a whole. Making learning personal is the backbone of successful teaching and learning, and is the single best solution we know of to change educational paradigms, but personalization is not to be confused with isolation.

The reason individualized curriculums are more effective is because of the same ideas that drive the frames of reference results—the lessons feel more *relevant* to the student—and the more relevant something is, the easier it is to learn. Educational methods designed to improve learning outcomes should allow for a degree of personalization in order to boost relevance, but the biggest barrier to doing this today is that it's difficult to efficiently *scale* personalized learning. Technology is beginning to change that; most important, we are finding creative solutions on smaller scales through adaptive learning software, so it's only a matter of time.

LEARNING STYLES

There are many ways to personalize learning. We'll see later how to do so through technology, but while we're still in the realm of psychology, one of the best ways that I've found of doing so is by assessing our individual *learning style*. The term is broadly used to refer to several similar theories based around the idea that everyone learns differently (something that has been proven both in sociological and biological research) and that these differences can be categorized to identify an individual's preferred style (or styles) of learning. For example, you may have heard someone referred to as being a "visual learner" or a "hands-on learner." While many different learning styles have been proposed, three of the more common ones found in most interpretations are *visual* (learning by seeing), *auditory* (learning by hearing), and *kinesthetic* (learning by touching or doing).

Proponents of learning styles believe that students learn best when taught through methods that match their dominant style. In an ideal classroom situation, teachers would recognize each student's learning style early, separate the class into groups of students who learn the same way, and then teach each group using its preferred method. In the real world, most teachers typically don't even know what the learning styles of their students are, much less have a system in place that differentiates between them.

One of the more common theories on learning styles is referred to as VAK, an acronym for *Visual, Auditory*, and *Kinesthetic*. Other variations of this are VAKT (which includes *Tactile*) or VARK (which includes *Reading*). The VAK model was first proposed by researcher Walter Burke Barbe and his colleagues in the 1970s. What their research found was that most people will learn things more easily if they're able to use their primary learning style to do so.[23] For example, if I'm a visual learner, I may be better able to learn by watching others do something. If I'm an auditory learner, I'd learn better by listening to an audiobook on the topic, and if I'm a kinesthetic learner, I would learn better by sitting down at the computer and physically doing it. Proponents of learning styles acknowledge that a combination of all these styles is almost always the best way to learn, but argue that there is typically one *preferred* method that would work better than the others if given the choice.

My youngest son, Jon, had been soaring along in school getting straight As, but then in fourth grade he mysteriously started to struggle. The school's education counselor had a conversation with him and then sent me a report that described him as "selfishly motivated" and a "troubled student." I was baffled. I've never been a fan of IQ tests (I believe curiosity is worth 100 IQ points!), but this time I went ahead and had Jon tested anyway, which didn't reveal any problem. But then his mother and I learned about a special kind of intellect testing called a "Structure of Intellect," which was subsequently given to him. The test, which measured what's called "learning modalities," revealed that Jon had an eye-muscle tracking problem, which made it more difficult for him to read. It also told us that Jon was a "visual-kinetic learner," meaning that he does not learn the same way that most people do—or the way our schools teach. Students like Jon learn best when there is something they can see, touch, and manipulate; whereas, as we have seen, our educational system is designed to teach via memorization, which leaves many youngsters like Jon out in the cold. The results of the test helped us include more visual-kinetic learning opportunities that supplemented his traditional school work, and I was thrilled to see that these changes made all the difference in the world in terms of his academic success.

He dropped out of high school, but would eventually go on to find a college in Bend, Oregon, that provided a match for his interests and learning styles, and he later graduated as an architect from Savannah College of Art and Design with honors. Today he has his own architectural firm, PACK. While his sister, Tiffany, had found success after identifying her individual "sweet spot," Jon found his own after identifying his individual learning style.

Observing Jon's experiences served as an early step in my coming to recognize the disparity between how schools teach and how students want and need to learn. In particular, for youngsters with any sort of learning disability or unique learning style, most school subjects present little more than a series of difficult hurdles. One of the primary reasons our educational system struggles to help kids realize their potential is because it simply isn't geared to recognize what's unique to each of them—including their learning style. To begin doing this, it must move toward more personalized learning in order to take advantage of this new realization about the differences we all have in the way we learn.

Somewhat related to learning styles, and an important concept you should be aware of, is the *theory of multiple intelligences*, proposed by psychologist and author Howard Gardner in his 1983 book *Frames of Mind*. This theory challenges the idea of there being a single type of intelligence that can be measured by any standardized test, including IQ tests. Gardner identifies not one, but eight different intelligences, and his theory challenges the common but false idea that everyone can learn the same concepts in the same way. As Gardner notes, "A belief in a single intelligence assumes that we have one central, all-purpose computer—and it determines how well we perform in every sector of life. In contrast, a belief in multiple intelligences assumes that we have a number of relatively autonomous computers—one that computes linguistic information, another spatial information, another musical information, and so on."[24] Whether we choose to look at students' learning style, type of intelligence, or both, what's most important when choosing how to better reach and teach them is that we must get away from the flawed notion that we're teaching *classes*, and understand that we're teaching *individuals* who just happen to be sitting in classes.

Once we have a better understanding of students' learning capabilities and the role personalized learning can play in meeting their needs, it's time to start locating their cognitive sweet spots. The *Zone of Proximal Development* (ZPD) was developed by psychologist Lev Vygotsky in the 1930s. ZPD was meant as a way of looking at the space between the things learners can do by themselves and those they need help with. The ZPD has a popular visual with three concentric circles representing different "zones" of learning. At the very center is the comfort zone (what a person can already do); just outside of that is the growth zone (where most learning takes place), and outside that is the panic zone (where a person cannot yet do things without help). The goal is to get, and keep, learners in their growth zones.

Similar to the motivational sweet spot discussed earlier (where passion and talent meet), the ZPD is kind of a cognitive sweet spot where, according to Vygotsky, the best learning takes place. For both sweet spots, the goal is to help students find their own personal cognitive sweet spot as well. If something is too easy or too difficult to learn, it can be a challenge, so the idea is to locate each child's zone and target it specifically.

COLLABORATIVE LEARNING

Some of the best learning that takes place isn't just personalized, but collaborative as well. In 1990, after seven years of teaching at Harvard, professor Eric Mazur was delivering clear, polished lectures and demonstrations, and getting high student evaluations for his introductory physics course, populated mainly by premed and engineering students. Then he discovered that his success as a teacher "was a complete illusion, a house of cards."

The epiphany was triggered by an article in the *American Journal of Physics* by Arizona State professor David Hestenes.[25] The author of the article had devised a very simple test, couched in everyday language, to check students' understanding of one of the most fundamental concepts of physics: force. He had administered the test to thousands of undergraduates in the southwestern United States. Astonishingly, the results showed that their introductory courses had taught the students "next to nothing. After a semester of physics, they still held the same misconceptions they had at the beginning of the term."

The students had improved at handling equations and formulas, he explains, but when it came to understanding "what the real meanings of these things are, they basically reverted to Aristotelian logic—thousands of years back." For example, they could recite Newton's Third Law and apply it to numerical problems, but when asked about a real-world event like a collision between a heavy truck and a light car, many firmly declared that the heavy truck exerts a larger force. (In fact, an object's weight is irrelevant to the force exerted.)

Mazur tried the test on his own students. Right at the start, a warning flag went up when one student raised her hand and asked, "How should I answer these questions—according to what *you* taught me, or how I usually think about these things?" To Mazur's consternation, the simple test of conceptual understanding showed that his students had not grasped the basic ideas of his physics course: two-thirds of them were modern Aristotelians.

Some soul searching followed. "That was a very discouraging moment," he says. "Was I not such a good teacher after all? Maybe I have dumb students in my class. There's something wrong with the test—it's a trick test! How hard it is to accept that the blame lies with yourself."

Finally, "I did something I had never done in my teaching career. I said, 'Why don't you discuss it with each other?'" As he described in the article where this story first appeared, "Immediately, the lecture hall was abuzz as 150 students started talking to each other in one-on-one conversations about the puzzling question."

"It was complete chaos," Mazur said. "But within three minutes, they had figured it out. That was very surprising to me—I had just spent *10 minutes* trying to explain this. But the class said, 'OK, we've got it, let's move on.'"

"Here's what happened," he continued. "When one student has the right answer and the other doesn't, the first one is more likely to convince the second—it's hard to talk someone into the wrong answer when they have the right one." More important, a fellow student is *more likely* to reach them than the professor—and this is the crux of the issue. "You're a student and you've only recently learned this, so you still know where you got hung up, because it's not that long ago that *you* were hung up on that very same thing." The professor got hung up on this point when he was seventeen, and he no longer remembers how difficult it was back then. He had lost the ability to understand what a beginning learner faces.

This innovative style of learning grew into "peer instruction" or "interactive learning," a pedagogical method that has spread far beyond physics and taken root on campuses nationally. In a recent year, Mazur gave nearly a hundred lectures on the subject at venues all around the world. He explained, in a 2012 *Harvard Magazine* article about his methods, "The students did well on textbook-style problems. They had a bag of tricks, formulas to apply. But that was solving problems by rote. They *floundered* on the simple word problems, which demanded a real understanding of the concepts behind the formulas."[26]

And he summed up what could be. "For teachers, the task is to work with students to take multidisciplinary standards-based content, connect it to what is happening in the world today, and translate it into an experience in which students make a difference in their community."

If the students will be entering careers where they will be challenged to solve real-world problems, what better way to get them started than to actively simulate the real world? With practice, their brains will be prepared to work in actual business settings years before they enter the workforce.

Once we're clear on our intended purpose of formal education, have a better understanding of learning, relatability, multiple intelligences, and learning styles, and can better personalize individual and collaborative learning experiences, then it's time to start making sure that the spaces that students can learn in, both physically and digitally, encourage all of this by design.

CHAPTER 6
SPACES

*If you wanted to design a learning
environment that was directly opposed to what
the brain is naturally good at doing,
you'd design a frickin' classroom.*
—JOHN MEDINA

After visiting hundreds of schools and classrooms around the world, I'm still amazed at just how traditional most of their physical spaces, and the things happening within them, seem to be. Students sit quietly (or not so quietly) in neatly aligned rows of desks, as a teacher lectures from the front of the class. But as we have seen, there are no standard learners, so they should not be forced to learn in standard classrooms, reading standard textbooks, and taking standardized tests. Digital natives have a desire to engage, socialize, share, and create things relevant to their lives, but often don't have access to dedicated learning environments that allow them to do these things. We must do a better job of ensuring the availability of purposefully built physical and digital learning spaces in which they can soar.

Educational futurist David Thornburg, in his book *Campfires in Cyberspace*, describes three types of primary learning spaces: the *campfire* (designed for one-to-many learning), the *watering hole* (designed for many-to-many learning), and the *cave* (designed for one-to-one learning).[27] Rather than trying to reinvent the wheel, I thought I'd instead share with you my own interpretation of Thornburg's learning spaces, to which I've added my own fourth space: the *mountaintop*. (Only after using this term for many years did I learn of Thornburg's most recent and similar addition to his spaces metaphor, *life*.) From my experience, the most effective schools and classrooms contain some form of all these spaces.

THE CAMPFIRE

It's no secret that storytelling is one of the most powerful ways of sharing information with others. No matter the content being shared, listeners are likely to remember the best of the lessons from these dramatic stories for the rest of their lives, as they go on to retell their own versions to future generations. One of the best places for hearing and telling stories historically has been over a campfire, where parents, grandparents, and camp leaders have shared their wisdom through a combination of fiction and real-life tales.

The campfire is an example of the one-to-many model, where typically one person speaks to many others at once. As Thornburg notes, the one-to-many model has been the most widely used form of learning space in schools for the past century. It's a teacher directly addressing students while walking excitedly around the classroom, or a guest speaker sharing their wisdom from the real world, helping to bring theories to life. When done right, the one-to-many model works well, but unfortunately more often than not, it's done wrong.

Lecturing motionless from the front of a class in a monotone voice as students fight to stay awake is also a form of the one-to-many model, but it's no campfire! I feel that it's not what's being shared that matters so much as it is the *way* that it's being shared. It's not content, it's craft, and employing a good story to convey information works well. An influential 1987 U.S. Department of Education study concluded that "even students with low motivation and weak academic skills are more likely to listen, read, write, and work hard in the context of storytelling."[28]

When stories are told, and rhetorical questions asked, in classroom environments designed to resemble the physical attributes of real campfires, the impact can be even greater. For example, rather than putting desks in rows, putting them in circles (either one big circle or several smaller group circles) where there's social reinforcement, and where everyone can see each other, might be a better option.

Technology now allows us to experience learning-based campfires in digital and virtual ways as well. One example is the use of video conferencing through the likes of Skype, iChat Video, iTunes U, or live YouTube streams. At Baldwin Elementary

School in Cambridge, Massachusetts, students have regular "visits" to campfires online through Skype, where engineers, scientists, and popular book authors share knowledge and experiences and hold Q&As in real time, even from the other side of the world!

Rewiring education doesn't mean abandoning traditional methods like one-to-many instruction; it just means ensuring that they're used in ways designed to *engage* students rather than put them to sleep.

THE WATERING HOLE

While the campfire is a learning space where an expert shares information with multiple learners, Thornburg's second example, the watering hole, is a space where people come together to share and collaborate with one another in a peer-to-peer manner. They can be both formal and informal. For example, think about the various spaces at one's job where people meet and share information and ideas. Breakrooms and even copy machines have been traditional places like this. In my HP days, we had designated areas in the halls where morning coffee and doughnuts were given out specifically for this purpose. Engineers, designers, and other team members from across departments would meet and chat each morning, discussing not just what we did or watched the night before, but what we were working on, sharing views and ideas. At Apple, Friday afternoon beer busts played that role.

What makes watering holes so important is that they offer an opportunity for those with different backgrounds, viewpoints, and personal anecdotes to share their ideas and thoughts with one another, allowing for the diversity of thought that's lacking in the one-to-many model.

In education, these types of watering holes, purposely designed to spark collaboration, are virtually nonexistent. Even at lunch, students typically just sit with their friends, chatting about anything *other* than school. At the university level, we often see the lower floor of libraries used as watering holes, but not so much in K–12, where they are instead considered quiet places where talking is forbidden—the exact opposite of what a watering hole should be.

Another difference between universities and K–12 in relation to watering holes is the very idea of collaboration itself. In college, collaboration is not only encouraged, it's usually required. When I was in high school, collaboration was called cheating. Every assigned project was a one-person project and there were no exceptions. This is beginning to change as the value of group projects and teamwork is slowly becoming more accepted, but I still visit many classrooms where the "every student for themselves" mentality persists. This is not preparing our children for real-world success, where collaboration and sharing will be required in both college and the workplace.

While informal watering holes could be created and encouraged outside of the school structure, they would be more effective as learning spaces if they were a formal part of the school itself. Most kids do not equate school with being very much fun, and the ones who do, more often than not, say that the fun part of school is seeing, talking to, and hanging out with their friends. The rare student will equate school with being fun due to the amount of learning going on. That's not likely to change, but what can change is how we design the learning process to *include* the ability to talk more with one another.

There's no reason that watering holes cannot be built directly into a school or classroom setting. The best-designed K–12 schools and classrooms that I've seen have intentionally carved out watering holes for learners, where students are asked to (1) share their own independent findings on the current lesson, (2) discover and explore in group-based settings, (3) elicit feedback from others, (4) become learners *and* teachers at the same time, and (5) make good use of technology.

Last, the popularity and recent explosion of digital watering holes, such as social networks like Facebook, Tumblr, and Snapchat, crowdsourcing sites like Wikipedia and Reddit, shared document editors like Apple's iWork and Google Docs, and multiplayer games like *World of Warcraft*, have shown us just how much people want and need to come together.

THE CAVE

Thornburg's third learning-space metaphor is the cave, where learners have the opportunity to spend time alone, writing, coding, researching, studying, thinking, meditating, and reflecting on the information they receive from other spaces. Rather than learning from or collaborating with others, the cave allows us to get in touch with our own inner thoughts as we attempt to make sense of the world and begin to integrate new information that we've learned with the things we already know.

Studies have consistently shown the need for metacognition—the awareness and understanding of one's own thought processes—in the learning process, which requires time for independent reflection.[29] But while educational experts often discuss the importance of student collaboration, group work, and teamwork, even if they haven't been effectively implemented, the cave is a learning space that's often forgotten and rarely factored into the design process, although it should be. It's important to note that cave spaces don't need to be enclosed, either—they just need to be *available*.

Sometimes, in libraries, you might notice desks put aside in corners—a form of public cave. These are often the first ones occupied and the hardest ones to get, because they offer a quiet sense of privacy in a noisy public world, where information can be transformed from external knowledge to internal understanding. Other natural cave spaces can include parks or trails where people can sit or walk alone, and beaches or lakes where people can relax and process their thoughts. These are the type of physical spaces schools and classrooms should build directly into their designs. I have seen specially designed tents and furniture used to provide cave-like appearances in both Australian and Mexican schools. The only limit is our imagination.

The challenge with using caves effectively is that we are asking the learner to use that space, and their time, to actively reflect on very specific topics, typically things that have just been taught to them. If the student finds the material being taught boring or irrelevant, getting them to reflect on it in their own time can be quite an obstacle to overcome. This is why all of the learning spaces are most effective when they coexist. If the material being taught is engaging enough through the use of campfire stories, and is being discussed and built upon by their friends at formal and informal watering holes, then the odds of them using cave time for active reflection increases dramatically.

Just as the previous learning spaces have both physical and digital representations, the cave does as well. Many technology products are specifically designed to foster a sense of individuality, allowing users to discover themselves in a variety of ways. Tablets, smartphones, and smart watches, for example, aren't just devices, but *platforms* built to host and encourage digital ecosystems where things can be invented or created at very personal levels. For students, this could mean using programs like Swift Playgrounds or ScratchJr. to learn to code and design their own app, or using iBooks Author or Adobe InDesign to write their own interactive books. Today, there are thousands of such cave-based opportunities available to students, often for free, allowing them to create and learn by doing little more than tapping, typing, and swiping.

THE MOUNTAINTOP

The final learning space metaphor is one I created as a follow-up to Thornburg's others: the *mountaintop*. This one is about bringing learning to life. Consider what it takes to successfully climb a mountain. While such an accomplishment certainly requires research, discussion, and reflection, eventually you're just going to have to try and climb the thing to really know whether or not you can. However, doing so requires that you have *access* to a mountain. This is why the mountain itself is the final learning space required for an ultimate understanding of any subject. Climbing the mountain is about learning by doing.

The true power of climbing a mountain comes from its built-in feedback system. Actively trying to do something provides instantaneous and constant feedback—a key part of learning that other spaces lack. Think about it in terms of testing. When climbing a mountain we know whether or not we have learned to do it. If we can climb the mountain, then the learning was a success. The test is our being able to do it at all. Now compare that to the testing taking place in schools. The only way we know whether or not we've learned something in school is by being tested on it, typically by answering multiple-choice questions. As discussed in chapter three ("Potential"), standardized tests do not measure learning; they measure one's ability to memorize and study for that kind of test. Only by doing things can we accurately measure if learning has taken place.

Unlike in other educational areas, where mistakes are often criticized or even punished (i.e., with grades on tests), mistakes during a mountain climb are not only encouraged, but required. As we saw in chapter four on motivation, when it comes to learning, mistakes should be thought of as valuable feedback and opportunities, not as errors deserving punishment. At Apple, for example, we believe that if mistakes aren't made early on, then we're not innovating enough. This mentality should become the norm in education as well. But in most K–12 schools and classrooms, hands-on real-world learning is completely missing. There are many reasons for this (organizational, financial, leadership-related, etc.), but a primary one is the lack of mountain spaces (i.e., makerspaces, entrepreneurship opportunities, etc.) dedicated to helping students climb.

Last, digital mountain climbing should play a critical role as well. Consider a student trying to teach herself to code with apps like Swift Playgrounds or ScratchJr., both designed specifically to teach kids how to code. It would be nearly impossible for her to learn by hearing a lecture and reading about coding, or discussing coding with her friends, or spending time alone reflecting upon coding. To learn to code, she needs to code, and that includes experiencing all of the mistakes and bugs that come along with it.

When both physical and digital spaces are made available to challenge them, climbers are able to scale the mountains. Once that happens you can be sure that true learning has taken place and will not likely be forgotten.

PUTTING IT ALL TOGETHER

While all of these spaces can take the form of various rooms and buildings, it's also important to know that even a single room, when used in different ways, can represent all of these learning spaces. It doesn't take a lot of room, but it does take a little creativity. I can't think of a better example of this than the story Marco Torres, a teacher, filmmaker, and close friend of mine, likes to tell about a former eleventh-grade student of his, David Peña.

David entered Marco's social studies classroom as a student who was highly interested in music. He was already in a local mariachi band and hoped to eventually become a music producer. One fall day, David had heard about a request for a guitar player for a music piece that Marco's film production studio needed for a movie it was working on. Since they made their own music for their movies, it wasn't uncommon for them to reach out into the school and ask for talented people. David, who had never recorded music before, decided to answer the call and stopped by the studio to record a guitar piece for the film. Marco loved it. But what he didn't realize at the time was that the tiny production studio had just become a nontraditional learning space where David now had an opportunity to excel, something he often was not good at in the traditional classroom setting.

To Marco's surprise, the very next day David showed up again in the production studio, this time wielding another instrument, and asked if he could record it. Marco let him, and the next day it happened again, and again, and again. Every time David returned he brought with him a different instrument to record. David was spending more after-school time at Marco's production studio than anywhere else. While there, Marco would teach David things directly (campfire), David would mingle and learn from others who were there (watering hole), and he would sometimes work by himself off in the corner of the room (cave). Marco was thrilled to see how excited David was whenever he was there. He was not just recording instruments, but *actively* engaged in the learning process at all levels.

Meanwhile, Marco's studio was also in the process of planning a major film festival for their student filmmaker program. Every year they focused on a specific theme, and that year the theme was Star Wars. The idea was to create a salute to Star Wars in the form of a parody. Marco decided to ask David, already a Star Wars fan, if he'd like to play the Star Wars theme with mariachi instruments, considering David apparently could already play *every* instrument in a mariachi band. David agreed and, for practice, Marco asked him to record another song, but this time to record all of the instruments on his own, one at a time. Having access to so many learning spaces at once helped prepare David to succeed. He was now using what he had been taught to create something real. He was climbing the *mountain* space, and the top was firmly in sight.

The song he created was a major achievement for David. "The song was amazing," Marco says, "It sounded like an entire orchestra of mariachi players all playing the Star Wars theme at once!" As David began to feel respect and recognition from Marco and others, his confidence rose. "As a teacher, you can imagine how exciting it was for me to see a student light up like that," Marco says. "To find their passion, have a voice, and, more importantly, have access to a studio, stage, and a community that helps him."

Eventually, George Lucas himself, the creator of Star Wars and director of the original film, and John Williams, the film's composer and conductor, ended up hearing David's *Star Wars Mariachi* tribute and were highly impressed. At one point, while at Lucasfilm, Lucas's production company, David even got a chance to play live for the legendary director.

The intentional design, creation, and implementation of learning spaces is a critical piece of successfully rewiring education, and will go a long way toward better meeting the needs of today's students. Once we start using these spaces in both physical, digital, and now *virtual* worlds, we empower students with a studio, a stage, and an audience, and we'll begin to see the classroom not in the traditional sense, but rather as a classroom without walls, without barriers, and without limits. It's up to us to create, and make available, these kinds of spaces, to allow students like David to learn and thrive.

Today, as a young adult, David Peña still performs and has achieved his goal of becoming a professional music producer. Just as impressively, he has now built a studio in his own house, a virtual mountaintop, where he records other local musicians, including ambitious students who wouldn't normally have access to such an extraordinary learning space.

CHAPTER 7

CHALLENGES

Never again is someone going to pay
you to give them answers they can
look up online. They'll only pay you to
solve problems that don't yet have answers.
—SETH GODIN

W hat TV show does education most resemble?"

Now that's *a challenge*, I thought, as I stood at the podium facing a group of around three hundred teachers, one of whom had asked the question from the darkness of the crowd.

"That's a good question," I said, buying myself a moment to think. "*Which* kids are we talking about? For some I think it would

be *America's Got Talent* or *Shark Tank*, but for others it would probably be more like *Survivor*."

Later that night I thought about that teacher's question again,
only this time in terms of what genre education resembles. Com-
edy? Horror? Again, I thought, the answer depends on which kids
we were talking about. But then I realized a major flaw in the answer
I had given earlier. The shows I named were *reality* shows. By contrast, over the years education has become more and more scripted.

Scripted shows are simpler for their participants, because they
are given the destination *and* shown a detailed roadmap (the script)
for getting there. They need only memorize the names of the
streets, so to speak, and follow a set of directions. Their action and
dialogue is predictable and their biggest challenge is memorizing
the information given up front. Reality shows are more challenging for participants, because while they're given the destination,
they are only told the general direction they need to go, rather
than being handed a roadmap. They must then work with others
along the way to figure out how to get there. Their actions and
dialogue are unpredictable and their biggest challenge is learning
from information gotten along the way. In education, students are
being prepared as actors for scripted shows, only to be cast into
the world of reality. In other words, what our kids are missing in
their academic studies is a healthy sense of *challenge*.

GOING OFF SCRIPT

Prior to the screenwriters' strike of 1988, television was mostly
dominated by scripted shows. But as the strike continued, networks
began looking for alternative programming they could air that

wouldn't have to rely on a set script. Some reality shows, such as *Real People* and *The Gong Show*, had succeeded, so the networks decided to take a chance and add more. Less than a decade later, the format had taken off and reality programming ruled the airwaves.

While much of reality programming is admittedly pretty bad, what many people find most interesting about it is the unpredictability inherent in the format. In scripted shows, the story takes a very clear path. Dialogue is memorized, delivered by actors, and overseen by directors and producers. There is no leeway for the actors to improvise or experiment.

Education is just like scripted television. Students play the role of the actors (and like real actors, often they are also struggling and getting burned out). The teachers are the directors, assigned to lead these actors through very strict, set-in-stone scripts (textbooks) crafted by writers (education policymakers) and approved by producers (politicians and administrators).

What's needed in education is a little *reality*. In reality TV there are no "actors," just real people—*individuals*, with their own real-world backgrounds, motivations, and talents. They have a general idea of what's going to happen in the show, but along the way surprises occur, learning takes place, and relationships are built. Just as in real life, they must learn to adapt to the realities of the situation at hand. The directors (teachers) are guides instead of bosses, and the job of the producers (policymakers) is to make sure that the overall goal is achieved—which, in education, would mean *learning*. The writer's job moves from writing a *standard* script to creating interesting *challenges* that are not meant to be followed step by step or word for word, but instead are meant to create interesting situations for the actors to respond to (and, in education, to *learn* from).

What would education look like if it were to become *challenge* based rather than *standard* based? "The whole thing about reality television to me," film director Steven Spielberg has said, "is really indicative of America saying we're not satisfied just *watching* television, we want you to discover us and put us in our own TV show. We want television to be about *us*, finally."

I submit that the same can be said about digital natives in our schools: they need education to be about *them*. They don't need a script telling them what to memorize, they need to be discovered and able to star in their *own* shows. The way I see it, we must stop trying to cast our kids as "better versions of ourselves," as Professor Todd Rose eloquently puts it in his book *The End of Average*. "We need to meet them where they are, engage them for who they are, and reject the myth of there being only one right way to succeed."

MYTHBUSTERS

There's one reality TV show in particular that I think gives us a good idea of what education might look like if it were designed to be both fun and challenging for learners. In 2003 a wildly successful science show called *MythBusters* premiered on the Discovery Channel and spent the next thirteen years teaching and entertaining viewers worldwide. Adam Savage and Jamie Hyneman, both special effects experts, were the show's hosts, and their job was to test common rumors, popular beliefs, and myths through cool science experiments. By the end of every segment the validity of each myth was rated as either *busted, plausible,* or *confirmed.* The show was highly engaging, and not just due to the charisma of the hosts. The audience's familiarity with the myths (which made the subject matter feel both personal and relevant) and the excitement of discovering the outcome of the experiments themselves both played integral roles in the show's success. Many of the myths the team tested came from fans of the show, allowing viewers to directly influence what was ultimately tested and increasing the sense of personal engagement.

It didn't take long before *MythBusters* became the most popular show on the channel, with everyone from kids to grandparents tuning in to see whether or not something they had heard was actually true. In each episode, before a myth was tested, a hand-drawn blueprint was shown, followed by a funny video explaining the myth and putting it in context. There was no script; instead, the team began with a rough idea about what they believed would happen, the type of experiment they were going to run, and the expected result. But what actually happened during each experiment was unknown until it was actually happening. After a show ran, if viewers could make a good case as to why the experiments were flawed, then the team would schedule another segment called "Myths Revisited," where they repeated the experiment based on the new feedback. Sometimes the fans would be proven right and the hosts would change or reverse their initial conclusions. This is exactly what rewiring education is all about: a series of challenging and relevant experiments that play off of preexisting experiences, where an engaging, and sometimes unpredictable, learning process ultimately leads to a clear understanding of the results.

There is no question that *MythBusters* was a show about learning, even if it had little to do with traditional education. What made it stand out was that it focused on highlighting the *process* of learning rather than just the outcomes. As Adam Savage stated in a recent interview, "Our engagement of the material is irrespective of whether or not we've obtained the goal which we've set out for ourselves." When asked why other similar science-based TV shows did not have the success they had, he said of the other programs, "The people in those shows aren't engaged enough with the material. The producers and writers may be, but the people on the ground doing it are not part of what's happening, not as involved and engaged with it, and that shows."

These "people on the ground" sound a lot like students in traditional classrooms. And in terms of allowing for failure? Hyneman explained, "The reality is, when you're watching us at work there, the eureka moments are those when we've failed. For me it just leads to more questions. And that's what this is all about, questions are the important thing. If we've done something and generated nothing but more questions, then that's a score."

MythBusters offers us a good example of how we can start keeping kids more engaged by adding a sense of challenge and fun to the learning process. It shows us that even traditional one-to-many systems, like television, have the potential to offer fun and interactive learning experiences by making little more than simple tweaks. Today, things like adaptive software, interactive videos, social media, smart devices, and immersive technology give us the power to implement tweaks like these into otherwise static systems like education, in ways that have never before been possible. Research has shown us for decades the potential of computer-based technology to transform the learning process, but getting school districts, schools, and teachers to actually incorporate it in transformative ways has been our biggest challenge to date.

KIDS CAN'T WAIT

Steve Jobs didn't have much formal education beyond high school, but part of his motivation at Apple was his recognition of the role that computers could play in revamping the teaching and learning process. When he was around ten years old, he saw his first computer and fell in love with it. Later, when he saw his first desktop computer at Hewlett-Packard, he immediately grasped its potential. "I thought if there was just one computer in every school, some of the kids would find it. It will change their lives," he said in a 1995 interview at the Computerworld Smithsonian Awards Program.[30] Later, early in Apple's history, he tried to bring that vision to life. In early 1978, Minnesota school kids were able to get access to five hundred Apple II computers through a deal Apple made with the Minnesota Education Computing Consortium, but it just wasn't enough. Bureaucratic roadblocks and red tape had slowed the process to a crawl, frustrating Steve to no end. "We realized that a whole generation of kids was going to go through school before they even got their first computer," he recalled. "But we thought—the kids can't wait." He wanted *all* kids to have access to computers, and he wanted to find a way to donate one to every school in America. It was this determination that led Apple to develop its *Kids Can't Wait* initiative.[31]

The idea behind Kids Can't Wait was to donate a computer to every school in America, but the reality was that we weren't very big yet and couldn't afford to do that outright. However, as Steve recalled in the same interview, "It turned out that there was a national law that said that if you donated a piece of scientific instrumentation or computer to a university for educational and research purposes, then you can take an extra tax deduction. We

thought that if we could apply that law, and enhance it a little bit
to extend it down to K–12, then we could give a hundred thousand computers away, one to each school in America. It would
cost our company ten million dollars, which was a lot of money
to us at that time, but we decided that we were willing to do that."

It was 1982 when Steve flew to Washington, DC, to lobby
Congress. He submitted a bill called H.R. 5573, the Computer
Equipment Contribution Act that, if passed, would have allowed
the tax break also to be applied to K–12 schools rather than just
universities. Unfortunately, the bill didn't pass. However, when
political leaders in California learned of this effort, they arranged
for Apple to implement Kids Can't Wait for the state's ten thousand schools. They also agreed to give Apple (and any other company) a tax break for the donations.

Not long after the deal was made, computers began arriving
at schools all across California, giving hundreds of thousands of
students access to one for the first time. Steve later called the success of the program "phenomenal" and spoke of it as one of the
most incredible things Apple had ever done. Even way back then
we knew that if students had access to the latest technologies and
were shown how to use them right, they could ultimately transform their learning process and help unlock their potential to succeed. We felt that all we needed was research to back that up.

THE ACOT STUDIES

It wasn't enough for Steve Jobs to personally set in motion the first
major efforts to drag our educational institutions into the digital
age. While Kids Can't Wait was designed as an initiative to get

a computer in every school, at Apple we knew we needed to do much more than that to really make an impact. We didn't just want to give kids access to technology; we wanted teachers and students to be able to use that technology to transform the entire learning process. So, in 1985, Apple began its first major educational research project, on how the needs of students could be better served through the use of technology. Rather than try to do it alone, we organized a research-and-development collaboration in an effort to determine what the best practices were for using technology in education and how it could be improved. The research study was called "Apple Classrooms of Tomorrow," or ACOT.[32]

Over the next decade, Apple and its collaborators—which included public school districts in California, Tennessee, and Ohio, as well as the National Science Foundation and academic researchers in colleges across the country—looked at how teachers' and students' everyday use of technology could affect the teaching and learning process. During this time, Apple and its collaborators developed ACOT classrooms called Teacher Development Centers, where we could test different technologies and curricula.[33] The goal was to train teachers to use technology in the classroom most effectively. The teachers would then return to their schools and districts as leaders in the area, teaching others to do the same. Hundreds of teachers representing dozens of states, various disciplines, and nearly every grade level participated in the program.

The key research results to come out of the ACOT classrooms were (1) most students don't learn well unless they are *engaged* on a personal level, as discussed in the previous chapters on motivation and learning, with relatability being very important; and (2) just as an inspirational teacher engages, so too does technology—when used as a way to transform teaching, as we'll look at in chapter thirteen.

The authors of the final research report wrote, "In ACOT classrooms, technology is viewed as a tool for learning and a medium for thinking, collaborating, and communicating." When technology was used in a variety of ways within a classroom, it significantly increased "the potential for learning, especially when it is used to support collaboration, information access, and the expression and representation of students' thoughts and ideas." Today that might sound like common sense, but in 1985 it was truly an innovative idea! We were thrilled with what we had learned from ACOT and used its research successfully to help transform the way technology in education, primarily via the personal computer, was used for the next two decades.[34]

By 2008 the world had changed. With the advent of the internet and with mobile computing on the rise, as well as personal and school-based technologies becoming more affordable, we launched a second round of ACOT studies titled "Apple Classrooms of Tomorrow—Today," or "ACOT²."[35] Going into the ACOT² research, we knew it wouldn't be enough just to point out the shortcomings in education without also offering practical solutions. So, this time the goals were more tactical. How could we help schools use technology to create the kind of learning environment today's students required, so they would find their classwork engaging, be motivated to stay in school, and be equipped to join the twenty-first-century workforce? Where ACOT was about gathering information, ACOT² research was aimed at figuring out what to do and how to do it. We wanted to create a specific action plan that would ensure the new digital generation of students would receive the type of education they needed to learn and stay in school.

ACOT^2's findings suggested that we needed to move away from a culture that considers learning to be an activity based on information *consumption*, to one that transforms learning in ways that are *relevant, creative, collaborative,* and *challenging*. It was this final addition of making learning challenging, but not too difficult, that would prove, well, *challenging*. We knew that if we were going to offer a solution that helped to improve education, we needed to figure out how to add a sense of challenge into the learning process, while simultaneously making sure it remained relevant, creative, and collaborative as well.

In other words, we needed to make learning something a bit more like reality TV, which is no small task. It was this dilemma that eventually led the ACOT team to reach out to the popular hosts of *MythBusters*. Working with them helped reinforce the importance of focusing on the learning *process* more than the result, and showed us how experiments could be used throughout the process to keep the learning relevant and challenging. I believe these lessons helped influence a lot of the things we subsequently did at Apple, even beyond our educational initiatives. It's one of the reasons why the iPad was released without an instruction manual (although there was an online version for those who wanted one)—it's just more fun to learn through experiment.

ACOT^2 offered an indictment of the way we have been teaching for decades. It wasn't instruction manuals, scripts, and roadmaps that were needed to teach content; it was ensuring that both the content *and* the process remained relevant, creative, collaborative, and challenging throughout. It was clear that we needed to rethink the status quo in terms of teaching and learning and move from a passive learning system to an active one. Thomas

Edison's educational film invention failed over a hundred years ago because he didn't listen to John Dewey's constructivist views on the importance of hands-on learning. At Apple, we wanted to learn from that mistake and ensure that our innovations had the chance to make a real impact on kids. The ACOT² research not only confirmed that we should be listening to constructivists like Dewey, Jean Piaget, Maria Montessori, and others; it also guided us on how to use technology to do it.

In an effort to bring the ACOT² findings to life, Apple worked with its teachers and partners to identify the best learning models, and fused them together with technology. The result: a new tech-supported pedagogy called *Challenge-Based Learning* (CBL) was born. The only question then was—would it work?

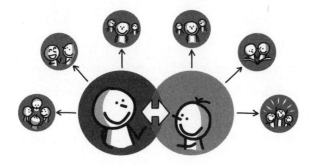

CHAPTER 8
CBL

I never teach my pupils,
I only attempt to provide the
conditions in which they can learn.
—ALBERT EINSTEIN

From outside appearances, Coppell High School, a suburban public school just outside of Dallas, looks just like any other ordinary, average high school. But if there's one thing I've learned in life, it's never to judge a book—or a school—by its cover. Take Coppell science teacher Jodie Deinhammer, for example. Jodie has been happily teaching at Coppell for over twenty years, and the things that take place within her Challenge-Based Learning (CBL) classroom are quickly becoming legendary.[36]

In 2015, Jodie's students were learning about the human body, and they came up with a challenge for themselves: they wanted to find ways of fighting childhood malnutrition, a common problem within their community. The "Big Idea" they came up with was a project called Health Without Borders, in which, under Jodie's guidance, they would use technology to create digital illustrations, texts, and multimedia projects as part of a series of interactive lessons for a global community.

Not only was the project itself an actual challenge, but throughout the process the students had other smaller challenges, in the form of "Essential Questions." Jodie's students learned a lot more than lessons about the human body and malnutrition; they also learned collaboration, teamwork, leadership, and project development; how to create new media, interview, research, present and speak publicly, budget, and use collaborative writing, editing, and illustration programs; and lessons in both sympathy and empathy—all within this single, month-long project. Most important, after the challenge ended, the students came away with a significant boost in their confidence levels, became closer friends, and, for the rest of their lives, will be able to look back at the things they made as something *they* created—something that now exists in the world that did not exist before.

PROJECTS: REWIRED

Challenge-Based Learning is an inquiry-based learning framework that poses individual and group-based challenges as a means of making learning relevant and engaging.[37] As a familiar frame of reference, consider for a moment the popular model known as *project-based learning* (PBL), in which teachers turn academic lessons into student-driven projects. PBL was inspired by the hands-on learning ideas of John Dewey and others, and turned into a loose framework that has gained in popularity over the past decade. The interactivity of PBL offers a tremendous improvement over the traditional lecture/textbook way of teaching and learning, but it isn't without its share of problems. Jodie recalls first learning about CBL while visiting a colleague at a school reunion in 2014. "Obviously I knew about PBL and had been using it for years with various degrees of success, and while I always tried to include technology in the PBL framework, sometimes it seemed forced and didn't make much sense," she remembers. "So, when I learned that CBL was designed specifically to address this issue, I was anxious to give it a try and haven't looked back since."

Rather than attempting to reinvent the wheel, CBL built upon the best parts of PBL, putting more emphasis on creating challenges and integrating technology throughout the process. The two frameworks both rely on hands-on projects to bring learning to life, but there are key differences. For example, students learning through PBL projects are often *assigned* that project, whereas those working on CBL challenges are encouraged to work together in designing their own. This tends to make the entire challenge more relevant for students, which increases their sense of ownership, buy-in, and motivation.

Another key difference comes in the way that technology is used. In PBL projects, technology isn't necessarily needed or even used at all, and where it is, it's most often used for simple information gathering on the internet. By contrast, in CBL challenges, technology is used throughout all stages of the process. It's not just a means of gathering information; it also provides various ways of communicating, collaborating, and boosting engagement. For example, where a PBL project may ask students to find a YouTube video to share as part of a slide presentation, a CBL challenge would ask them to *create* a YouTube video to share as part of a live simulation. Where a PBL project may ask students to read a blog and take notes, a CBL challenge would have the students cocreate their own vlog (video blog), while using digital annotation tools to embed notes within it. CBL challenges aim to move kids away from being just consumers of content, and toward being its producers and creators, just as Jodie's class did by creating their multimedia projects.

A third major difference is that PBL is frequently limited to ideas and projects done within the classroom or school environment, whereas CBL asks learners to actively involve the broader communities, and to design and implement solutions to problems that directly affect them. In Jodie's class, childhood malnutrition was chosen precisely because it was a major concern within their own community. I realize that CBL isn't the only solution to making learning more engaging and meaningful to digital natives, but it does a really good job of it, just as it was designed to do.

THE CBL FRAMEWORK

While Challenge-Based Learning was born out of Apple's ACOT[2] research, it was designed and developed by a team of professional educators and engineers that I put together.[38] What we were trying to do was design a highly flexible model of teaching that would make the process of learning more relevant, creative, collaborative, and challenging for digital natives.

One of the people recruited to work on ACOT² was a man with a rather diverse background. Mark Nichols had worked as a middle-school teacher, soccer coach, and wilderness guide. He had done software development, spent time working at a school on an Apache reservation, and worked for a television station that broadcasts reality shows. It was this work on TV that really had him thinking about what the learning process might be like if it had more of a reality TV–like kick to it. That curiosity naturally led him to our CBL development team, where he became quite an asset. "We looked at television cooking shows and fashion shows, and began to recognize a formula," Mark said. "They all started with some kind of a challenge, and the contestants had to produce something that fit the rules." It was true; the reality TV shows were almost always built around the power of a challenge, like we wanted with CBL.

In CBL, students tackle projects of their choosing, related to one or more course subjects, which is turned into a group-based challenge. It's an engaging, multidisciplinary approach, where kids can leverage the technology they use in their daily lives—mobile phones, computers, the internet—in an effort to find and develop solutions to real-life problems. While I've always understood the importance of relevancy in the learning process, it wasn't until I began working on the challenge-based learning framework, and witnessed the amazing results, that I saw with my own eyes the true potential of learning-by-doing. I have now seen classrooms full of students, just like Jodie's, being transformed into physical/digital mountain spaces.

The CBL framework consists of three distinct phases. In phase one, the teacher guides the students in coming up with a problem they want to solve that's related to whatever the academic topic happens to be. Once a problem is chosen, they then work collaboratively to come up with a broad "Big Idea," which represents a way for them, as a class, to potentially solve the problem. In Jodie's example, the Big Idea was the creation of the multimedia lessons students would share with others. The problem and Big Idea are often based on a current issue that is harming a learner's own school or community. It's not required, but the more *relatability* it has for the students, I have found, the bigger the impact will be for them. It could be something as large as poverty, homelessness, or climate change, or something as small as their school not offering healthy foods.

Once the problem (and a general Big Idea to solve it) has been decided upon, phase two begins where the teacher and students break the problem down into smaller "Essential Questions." The goal of these questions is to make the Big Idea more manageable, and personalize it so that its relevance becomes more immediate. Essential Questions include things like *How might we do this particular thing? What might the obstacles be and how might we get around them? How will all of this actually work?*

"One of the most difficult parts of implementing CBL is often at the start of a project, when students are asked to come up with Essential Questions," Jodie says. "They often don't know where to start. So, I've created a separate question for challenging both my students and myself when thinking about these things: *How can we make a difference in our society?* I ask them. Once we have an answer to that, then the other questions just seem to come naturally." Essential Questions trigger various investigations by the students, which include working alone and in teams, to plan, research, interview, take field trips, and more, in an effort to find the answers. While much of the investigation phase takes place outside of the four walls of the classroom, all Thornburg's learning spaces, as well as mountain spaces, are typically used in some fashion. As the teacher continues to guide and facilitate the investigations, they eventually culminate in a clear Action Plan.

The Action Plan comes as part of CBL's third phase, where students start acting on their findings. They use elements of the design cycle (prototype, test, and refine) to come up with evidence-based solutions, which are then implemented either within the school, the broader community, or somewhere else in the world entirely through online tools. Various interactive technologies can be used throughout the process. Jodie's class, for example, used things like audio and video recordings, blogging, social media, crowdsourcing, and digital publishing.

Throughout the course of the challenge, students are constantly guided, frequently asked "why?", and expected to think critically about everything they're doing. They keep written records (either by hand or digitally) in the form of reflections during each phase, which give teachers and parents an active account of what's being learned and plenty of opportunities to discuss it.

Since the CBL framework is flexible by design, teachers can make changes at any point along the way that fit the needs of their class, lesson, or even an individual student. CBL was designed specifically to not be yet another system forced on teachers who already have too much to do. Instead, it's meant to provide a framework, or structure, for many of the things teachers are already doing. Think of it as a way to fuse the best elements of teaching with the best elements of current technology. It's this inherent flexibility that allows CBL to be useful in almost any situation, even teaching content for state standards.[39]

Whenever I find myself trying to describe CBL to others in a way that's memorable, I like to use a "shorthand" method I learned from a friend of mine in Mexico, Alphonso Roma Jr., who has been committed to improving education for many years. The way he describes CBL is: Feel, Imagine, Do, Share. In other words, what do you feel? Can you imagine a solution? Now go solve the problem and then share the solution with the world.

MAPPING TO STANDARDS

There is sometimes pushback by teachers who are considering implementing an inquiry-based learning framework like CBL. While they will typically agree that teaching in a relevant, creative, collaborative, and challenging framework is ideal, they are still concerned that they won't be able to implement it when their administrators expect them to "teach to the test." Even great teachers, with enormous potential, find that they cannot teach their students the way they know they need to without the risk of punishment. This is why it's important for all educational frameworks to be able to map directly to the appropriate state standards. Luckily, CBL has the ability to do just that.

Let's say, for example, that you're a fourth-grade social studies teacher in California, and statewide standards indicate that your students must be well-versed in California history. Traditional test prep for this kind of assignment would require students to read small sections of California history (the minimum amount of content the publishers are required to create in order to sell textbooks in the state), memorize some pointless facts, take a few quizzes, possibly do a project to build a mission out of sugar cubes, and then finally sit down to take the exam. But what could a teacher using the CBL framework do differently?

One idea might be to have the class pretend they are William Randolph Hearst and plan to throw a hypothetical award dinner at the Hearst castle in San Simeon, California, for the most influential people in the state's history. The kids would be responsible for deciding who to invite, or not invite, to this dinner. They are given no other instructions. What this does is force the students working in teams to do various types of research, which would include online searches, virtual and in-person library and museum trips, interviews, and more. Because they also have to decide which famous historical Californians *not* to invite, they know they'll need to be able to justify why these people weren't invited. By asking Essential Questions related to the Big Idea, collectively the students are able to pore through the pros and cons of hundreds of potential invitees, learning more about the history of California, and in a more fun way, than they ever would have through a textbook.

An additional sub-challenge might be if the teacher asks the students to determine the seating chart for the individuals invited to the dinner. They could even write scripts of conversations that might take place between attendees, record a live version of the entire encounter, and turn it into a California history video, totally student-made, with new and improved conversations added every year. This could then be uploaded online (and constantly added to) and used by schools across the state to better help *other* students learn the history, helping to solve the challenge of doing so in ways that both entertain and inform. With a little creativity, the possibilities of tying CBL challenges to state standards are endless, as is its ability to adapt from one class to the next.

HEALTH WITHOUT BORDERS

A year after Jodie's students had begun their Health Without Borders project, they all moved on to higher grades and were replaced by an all-new class. Once the new class, which had heard about the successful project, reached the same lesson on the human body, they decided that they wanted to continue working on, and try to improve upon, the original Health Without Borders project. The new students decided to build upon the interactive media projects of the earlier students by putting together their own book. They updated the previous class's research, collaborated on an outline for various sections and chapters, and then worked together to create an impressive collection of supporting materials that included original drawings and photographs and 3D models of organs that they digitally created. It was a massive effort that called upon them to go above and beyond their in-class work, which they did willingly and happily.

When their project was done, the students not only presented it to the class and the school, but they also posted it online as part of an iTunes course. Today that course has over 50,000 subscribers, their book has been downloaded over 12,000 times, and the kids that worked on both the original and the revised project have been contacted by other kids from twenty-four different countries with praise, questions, and feedback.

Another incredible success story that came out of this project is that of a young student who had put a lot of work into the book's digital illustrations. She'd had no previous experience doing this type of illustrations, but thought that it sounded cool and wanted to give it a try. Today, she is happily employed as a professional medical illustrator—not because she took a course at her school on illustration, but solely due to the experience of finding her talent and passion as part of a single CBL project. Giving students the chance to explore the world outside of their comfort zone lets them discover and use talents they often don't even realize they have.

As amazing as the Health Without Borders story is, I can't necessarily call it "extraordinary"—because in Jodie's class, through CBL, these types of incredible stories have become downright ordinary. Another one of Jodie's classes put together a book on endangered animals that they researched by hanging out with them at the zoo and reaching out to other kids in Thailand to ask questions about elephants. Through interpretation software they exchanged messages with people at the Sumatran tiger facility in Cambodia and at a vulture program in Central Africa, and FaceTimed with a penguin rescue effort in Cape Town, South Africa. The zoo that they visited even threw a public release party for the book and its student authors, photographers, and illustrators. "Those kids have the pride of being published authors," Jodie says. "And they've gained a vision and understanding of conservation that they could never have gained from class lectures or reading online material."

MAKING A DIFFERENCE

My colleagues and I, both inside and outside of Apple, had a lot to do with the development of CBL, which is why I'm so passionate about it. However, don't think that I have an ulterior motive. CBL is a free and open framework that anyone can use, including teachers, parents, students, or administrators. Apple products or services are not essential to use CBL and there are no proprietary ideas or subscriptions. My passion for CBL, and my belief in its viability as a means of rewiring education, is genuine. I know it works, because I see it making a difference in classrooms across the country. Jodie Deinhammer's classes perfectly highlight its potential to promote active learning through relevant, creative, collaborative, and challenging lessons. Even so, just giving teachers knowledge of CBL and the skills to implement it isn't enough— to *really* make a difference, we also need time and resources and pedagogical changes to the system. Luckily, once again, technology offers answers.

CHAPTER 9
ACCESS

The future has arrived—
it's just not evenly distributed yet.
—WILLIAM GIBSON

I t began on a cool fall evening in October 2014, in a remote section of Coachella Valley, California. A school bus rolled to a stop in front of a house to drop off its last few students for the day. Nothing out of the ordinary there. But then the drivers did something strange. Rather than return the buses to their designated lots, they parked them in some of the poorest communities of the Coachella Valley Unified School District (CVUSD). The drivers then got out and went home, leaving the school buses unattended.

While there wasn't anything notably distinguishable about these buses from the outside, glancing inside would have revealed something quite extraordinary. The buses had been turned into mobile hotspots. Along with the thousands of iPads that had been provided to Coachella Valley's students, these buses were about to give some of America's poorest students their first-ever access to the internet. From that day on, Coachella Valley school buses would not just bring home kids, they would bring home iPad and internet *access*.

"We call it 'Wi-Fi on Wheels,'" Dr. Darryl Adams announced proudly during an interview at the time. "And it's going to change the lives of our kids in ways they can't even imagine."[40]

Adams, a former Los Angeles Teacher of the Year turned district superintendent, was brought in to shake things up at Coachella Valley Schools, which had the unfortunate distinction of being one of the poorest districts in the entire country. Many of its communities are in very rural areas, and of their 20,000 students, the luckiest ones lived in shabby trailer parks, while other, not-so-lucky ones often spent nights sleeping in alleys, parks, and abandoned railroad cars. With a 94 percent poverty rate, few CVUSD parents had their own cars, much less their own houses. Public transportation was spotty at best. Few people had computers, and the luxury of the internet was nearly unthinkable. All of this left most students with no way of accessing the most basic news, information, and services.

One of the first things Adams wanted to do as superintendent was to change this. "Without access," he said, "there are few opportunities to succeed in anything." There had to be a way to get these families access to the internet and provide them with some of the same basic opportunities that more fortunate kids had. The question was, *how?*

Darryl Adams is a fun and highly creative man. He once taught music to high school students among the bright lights of Los Angeles, and now called himself the "Rock and Roll Superintendent." He found that it made people smile—which is not always easy to do for people who are struggling just to survive. But the name also told people something else about him. It told them that Adams was *different*, and that he wasn't interested in falling in line with tradition. He was someone who thought outside the box, and it was this thinking that led him to the idea of putting solar-powered Wi-Fi hotspots on school buses and leaving them scattered throughout the communities they served.

It didn't take Adams long to convince the school board and voters to use bond funding to start a Mobile Learning Initiative, which included free iPads for every student in the district along with the Wi-Fi on Wheels program. "We wanted to ensure that students had 24/7 access to the internet," Adams said. "Learning does not stop at the end of the day." Along with the iPads and internet, a new curriculum was also added that allowed students to begin preparing for specific careers like engineering, aviation, science, and sports.

The results? Within a year attendance rates went up, student motivation and engagement increased, and the graduation rate grew from 70 percent to 80 percent. Adams went on to be recognized by President Obama as one of the Top 100 Innovative Superintendents in America and by the Center for Digital Education as one of its Top 30 Technologists, Transformers, & Trailblazers in America. But as nice as those recognitions are, it doesn't take long for Adams, when asked about them, to wave them off and focus back on his true passion—his students. "These kids are coding now and flying drones," he said with a smile.

It's stories like this one that help keep the dream of educational equity alive and well, especially in the digital age. When I speak, I frequently propose that to rewire education, one of the things we need in education today is a new set of principles that I refer to as the "21st Century ABCs of Learning": Access, Build, and Code.

ACCESS TO OPPORTUNITY

It doesn't matter how good a technology is if those whom it's intended to help don't have access to it. In terms of the 21st Century ABCs of Learning, *access* means access to things like extraordinary teachers, great schools, and transformative technologies. But first and foremost, it means access to fast and reliable internet. The problems that plagued Coachella Valley's schools are not isolated. While most middle- and upper-class homes in America today have at least one computer and broadband internet access, the same is not yet true for those in our poorest communities. Thousands of students all over the country still don't have access to adequate computers or internet, making it nearly impossible for them to succeed in *today's* world, much less tomorrow's.

Things are starting to change, albeit slowly. The cost of computers and internet access continues to drop, and municipal wireless networks, which blanket entire cities with free Wi-Fi, are becoming more popular. Google's *Project X*, its secretive research and development program, is also developing "Project Loon," where massive, high-altitude balloons are being designed to fly overhead and beam down free wireless to millions of people below.[41]

Other positive trends and innovations across the country are helping improve access to technology as well. For example, one of Apple's largest current philanthropic efforts is a $100 million pledge to help ensure the success of the national ConnectED initiative. As CEO Tim Cook explained, "We've always believed that education is a great equalizer, a powerful force for change, for good, but we're keenly aware that not every school can have this impact. That's why we're so deeply committed to ConnectED, a national initiative combining government and leading technology companies to bring our technologies to underserved schools."

The ConnectED program was introduced in June 2013 by President Obama as a massive new educational technology program that sought to empower teachers with the best technology and training, and empower students through personalized, digital content. As vice president of education, I was blessed to be Apple's representative in the program. Aside from Apple, dozens of other major tech companies collaborated with us on the effort, including Microsoft, Sprint, Verizon, and Adobe. The stated goal of ConnectED was to ensure that "99% of American students had access to next-generation broadband by 2018."[42]

As an early supporter of ConnectED, Apple donated technology and training to 114 underserved schools across twenty-nine states, committing to providing a free iPad for every student, a free iPad and iMac for every teacher, and LCD screens and Apple TVs for every classroom. However, based on some of the things we learned from our ACOT research, we knew that just handing over technology to schools and expecting them to intuitively know how to use it just doesn't work. Instead, to supplement our physical donations, we committed to providing planning, training, and ongoing professional development and support. Tech companies like Google, Microsoft, Facebook, Adobe, and others also pitched in to ensure that our technologies and services reached those who needed them most.

Not long after the program began, tens of thousands of students who previously had no access to quality technology were tapping, swiping, creating, sharing, and learning in ways they never thought possible. Within the first two years over 50,000 students had gained direct internet access.[43]

NO PANACEA

Training and support to go with the technology, as we've seen, is key in making a difference. Technology, in and of itself, is not a panacea for solving problems, including those related to education.

When it comes to education, there are few things for which Apple gets more press (both good and bad) than school districts buying iPads for their students. Even though the necessity of access to technology is widely agreed upon, whenever there is a large effort to put that access in the hands of many students at once, it invariably leads to controversy. This typically comes in the form of full-court press attacks, most often directed at school leaders, but also at the companies providing the technology. When purchases don't provide the desired results as quickly as expected, it doesn't take long before fingers start pointing. And as a result of misunderstandings in situations like these, fewer kids get access to the technologies they need to succeed.

Not long ago a large school district decided to begin moving toward a fully digital curriculum. We were excited that they had chosen iPads as the core technology, but were concerned by the fact that they were purchasing them with little forethought and essentially handing them out to the teachers and students like Christmas presents, with no training or support. Almost immediately problems emerged, and the entire initiative was widely labeled as a disaster. The experience bolstered the flawed ideas that (1) technology isn't the way to solve problems in education, and (2) tech companies are more a part of the problem than the solution.

When Apple delivers iPads to school districts, optional teacher training and support services are offered. Unfortunately, not every district takes advantage of these, and without being trained to use technology in the right ways, teachers will often end up using it as a means of efficiency, rather than transformation. They may download an eBook, for example, or a flash card game, simply transferring the same learning process they were using before from a non-tech source (i.e., a book or worksheet) to the iPad. Later, when the students are tested, the findings rightfully conclude that there really isn't much difference between learning with technology and learning without it. When these results go public, they're seen as evidence that the benefits of technology for student learning are limited. Context has a history of not going public and often doesn't play nicely with dramatic sound bites.

In the case of the large school district just mentioned, their leadership knew the iPads could significantly boost the learning potential of the city's low-income students. Many of these students had little to no access to technology, and were being left behind their more affluent neighbors in access to technology and, because of that, in how much they were learning. This led to a sense of urgency in delivering the iPads that ultimately led them to forgo the proper setup, prep, and teacher trainings. Principals were not given enough time to prepare, and key faculty, staff, and teachers were left out of the planning process, leaving them overwhelmed and frustrated. It was this lack of collaboration and preparation that doomed the program from the start.

Not long after the program began, the superintendent resigned, and public blame for the program's failings shifted from district decisions, including the lack of digital content, to the technology itself. Comparisons between the iPad and a competitor's low-end laptop began making the rounds. "The laptop cost significantly less," it was argued at the time. "It should have been considered instead of the iPad!" But a bare-bones laptop, offering little more than internet access, is not really comparable to a tablet packed with an ecosystem of interactive apps.

The problems with this district's initiative stemmed from a severe lack of planning and execution. However, when those pieces of the puzzle are there, the addition of technology almost always leads to extraordinary outcomes, just as they did for Darryl Adams in Coachella.

ONLINE LEARNING

Another big recent change in access has been the emergence of online learning. Massive open online courses (MOOCs)—programs and classes taken on the internet—are perhaps the most prominent of these. Aimed mostly at adult learners so far, MOOCs come in many different variations and can cover just about any topic in the world. Despite a rocky start (due to overly optimistic expectations),

MOOCs have grown significantly over the past five years, evolving from virtual classrooms to self-paced, on-demand lessons students can take in their own time. Some MOOCs work with colleges and professional programs to offer for-credit courses, while others offer stand-alone classes designed for those who just want to learn more about things. Some MOOCs cost money, either per class taken, by the hour, or in return for receiving specific credentials at the end of the course, but others are free for anyone to take. Udacity, Coursera, and Harvard/MIT's edX have led the way in expanding this still emerging field.[44]

But MOOCs aren't for everyone. Structured online learning can take an incredible amount of self-discipline and motivation—often missing from struggling students—meaning MOOCs alone, even when they become more available for K–12 students, may not be an effective solution for teaching them. A mistake many MOOCs make is simply moving lecture content online, without bothering to create a new context for online learning. Turning a lecture into a video and posting it online is the lowest possible form of educational technology and has nothing to do with truly rewiring education. I do believe, however, that all learners could benefit from using interactive and well-designed online lessons to complement, although not replace, in-person, face-to-face learning, in what's often referred to as a *blended learning* approach.[45]

Khan Academy is an online school that specializes in creating free and easy-to-understand learning videos on a wide variety of topics. Sal Khan founded the nonprofit as a simple YouTube channel in 2006, onto which he uploaded a few videos of him explaining some math concepts for a cousin. Sal's videos were effective at simplifying otherwise complex ideas, and soon others began finding and sharing them. A *lot* of others. Before long hundreds, and then thousands, of people were learning math from these three- to five-minute videos. Eventually, as Sal kept making more videos, he decided to become more formalized. Khan Academy was born, and quickly outgrew being a YouTube channel. As the overwhelming demands for these short videos outgrew Sal's capability to make them, he expanded and began hiring others who were just as adept at simplifying complex concepts. By expanding the topics covered to things beyond math, it drove hundreds of thousands more people to the site. At its peak, Khan Academy had nearly 10 million active students, making it the largest distributor of educational content on the planet.[46]

Sal Khan, meanwhile, had moved out of obscurity and into the realm of legend. In 2012, *Time* magazine named him one of the 100 Most Influential People in the World. But the fame never went to Sal's head; he remains just as humble and motivated as he was when he put up those few little math videos for his cousin. Even with all of Khan Academy's success, Sal knew that online learning alone wasn't enough. In 2016, Sal opened his first Khan Lab School, a physical school attached to the Khan Academy offices that merged the best parts of the online school with the best practices of in-person teaching and learning.[47] I met with Sal not long after the Lab School was opened and got a chance to take a tour, including meeting some of the school's kids, teachers, and parents. I was truly impressed at how well they were able to blend the online and offline learning experiences. Today, Sal has added a wide range of material to both Khan Academy and his lab school, including coaches (tutors), live chats, interviews, games, challenges, and more.

APPLE CAMP

Initiatives and new innovations like ConnectED and online learning are important, but to truly achieve access for all learners, we have to start thinking differently. Access to technology and innovative learning opportunities shouldn't depend on schools or having Wi-Fi at home.

We already know learning opportunities can be provided in plenty of places besides schools and homes, such as libraries, museums, and community centers. But retail stores?

One of my key initiatives in 2002 was to work with our retail stores. I couldn't help but notice how many parents would bring their kids with them into Apple Stores while they shopped. The kids were naturally drawn to the games on the display computers. Most Apple Stores had already created a small area where kids could sit and play, but I believed that Apple was missing out on an opportunity. "What if, instead of playing games and watching videos, kids could actually learn to create them right there in the stores?" I wondered.

Before long we started a new program called "School Nights," where Apple allowed local schools to host an evening in the store to showcase their students' work. Apple Summer Camps—specialty camps where kids eight to twelve years old could learn to write and illustrate their own books, make their own short films, and program robots—soon followed.

I felt so strongly that retail could play a crucial role in our education strategy that I transferred my Director of Education Marketing, Kris Bazan, to the retail division. As every Apple store in the world began to offer these specialty camps, Kris partnered with third-party educational developers like Tynker, Hopscotch, and Sphero to help develop the curriculum. She also gathered input from all relevant stakeholders, including teachers and parents, throughout the entire design, development, and roll-out process, and added coding to the camp curriculum. Kris's latest program is "Teacher Tuesdays," where teachers connect with other teachers to collaborate and learn new skills through hands-on projects. They explore unique ways to engage students ages five and up, manage their classrooms, and create learning activities using iPads.

Today thousands of students have begun learning to code in Apple retail stores. I believe that we must think beyond the walls of our schools and homes when it comes to giving kids the access they need. After- and before-school programs, summer programs, library programs, museum programs, YMCA programs, and yes, even programs placed right in the middle of retail stores are all good examples of ways that we can provide access and opportunities to kids no matter where they are.

BEYOND TECHNOLOGY

When talking about ensuring that students have access and opportunity in the context of rewiring education, I spend a lot of time discussing things related to technology, but I want to be clear that technology is only one piece of a very complex puzzle. Having access to it can certainly help to unlock students' potential, but it has a much better chance of doing so if other pieces are in place as well. Luckily, many of us who work in tech and are passionate about education know this and try to find ways to ensure students also have access to the things they need beyond technology.

Many people may not know the name Priscilla Chan yet, but she is quietly making a powerful impact on kids by blurring the lines between her two biggest passions: education and health care. While attending Harvard in 2007 as a biology major, Chan began mentoring disadvantaged students in a nearby community plagued by poverty, crime, and gang activity. It was there that she saw first-hand just how much living under these conditions harms children.

In an interview with the *San Jose Mercury News*, she recalled working with a girl who had just had her front teeth knocked out, and another time seeing a child with blood on his face after he was brutally attacked. "I realized that my homework help was going to be completely futile if these kids couldn't be healthy, safe, and happy in the place where they lived," she said. "That really drives a lot of what I decided to do in my life and career."

After college, Chan (the first college graduate in her family) spent a year teaching science to fourth and fifth graders. She went on to earn her pediatric medical degree in 2012, the same year that she and her husband, Facebook founder and CEO Mark Zuckerberg, were married. But even as she suddenly found herself wealthy, she never lost her passion for kids and continued to work as a pediatrician at a major hospital. She also never forgot the lessons she learned while mentoring, and vowed to dedicate her life to making a difference in kids' lives.

Chan and Zuckerberg met nine years prior to their getting married, while standing in a bathroom line at a pre-Facebook fraternity party. Chan eventually got Zuckerberg interested enough in educational issues to cofound a nonprofit, Startup: Education, a grant-making foundation dedicated to helping improve access to high-quality education for all students. In 2010, the couple began by pledging $100 million to help improve troubled schools in Newark, New Jersey. The foundation made other smaller donations over the next few years and then, in 2014, donated another $120 million to San Francisco Bay Area schools.

But for Chan, giving money away wasn't enough. She could never get the faces and stories of those kids that she mentored out of her head. She wanted a more active role in the process of ensuring that kids got the help that they needed. In October 2015, Chan announced that she would also be opening a free private school dedicated to providing "whole child" support for its students. Most important to Chan, the school would focus just as much on health as it did academics, what she and Zuckerberg refer to as an "integrated health and education model." Chan understood that a traditional school that only focused on academics, while ignoring the things that help lead to academic success, was not going to work. She needed to find a way to do it right—to bring all of the pieces together.

One month after announcing The Primary School (TPS), Priscilla Chan gave birth to her and Zuckerberg's first child, a baby girl named Max. This was a particularly emotional moment for the couple, because they had tried and miscarried more than once. This time they got their baby. To celebrate the joyous occasion, the couple made the public announcement that they were pledging 99 percent of their shares in Facebook to health and educational charities—at the time of their announcement worth over $45 billion. In the meantime, they had a school to open.

TPS launched in August 2016 and differs from traditional schools in several key ways. Rather than starting with six-year-old kindergartners, the full-time school is open to preschoolers through eighth graders. They also partner with primary care providers to ensure children get the health care they need. In terms of staffing, TPS has a full-time medical director who coordinates with primary care providers and also trains teachers and parent coaches to support health needs. These individuals collaborate with each other and with parents to create "growth plans" for students that measure and track their health, education, and social-emotional progress over time. In describing itself online the company notes, "Our approach integrates primary education and primary care, effectively braiding together education, health, and family support services starting at birth. In doing so, TPS will expand the traditional definition of 'school' in order to prepare all children to succeed in college, career, and life."

For Chan, putting the pieces together to improve education means bringing together all stakeholders in the child's well-being, including teachers, health coaches, parents, doctors, community leaders, and community members. While it's still too early to see the results of this effort, Chan is clearly embracing one of the most important lessons in rewiring education: that to succeed, we must find ways of merging multiple dimensions—not just academics, but health care, psychology, and technology.[48]

So, although ensuring that all kids have access to key technologies is critical, we must also ensure that they have equal access and opportunities in other key areas as well. There are no simple, one-dimensional fixes in a system as complex as education.

CHAPTER 10

BUILD

What we learn to do,
we learn by doing.
—THOMAS JEFFERSON

O nce we're able to better ensure that all students have access to key technologies, among other things, it's time to start looking at what students are actually able to *do* with this access. This is where the second letter of my 21st Century ABCs of Learning comes in: "B" for *build.*

"It's important to teach problem-solving, and teach to the *problem* and not the tools," entrepreneur Elon Musk said in an interview with Beijing TV.[49] In 2015, Musk, the visionary founder of Tesla and SpaceX, pulled all five of his sons out of an exclusive private school because, he felt, it was unable to meet their twenty-first-century needs. Instead of embarking on a long search to find another school that could, Musk chose instead to open his own. He transformed a rarely used house he owned into Ad Astra, a small school tasked with teaching students in ways that better match their own unique gifts.

At Ad Astra, Latin for "to the stars," there were no grades, and the school's mission was to cater directly to each student's skill set and passion. Most important, Musk insisted that the school be designed around learning by *doing*.

"Let's say you're trying to teach people about how engines work," he explained in the interview. "A more traditional approach would be saying, 'We're going to teach all about screwdrivers and wrenches.' But this is a very difficult way to do it. A much better way would be, 'Here's the engine. Now let's take it apart. How are we going to take it apart? Oh, you need a screwdriver.' It's then that two important things happen: the relevance of the tools becomes apparent, and the students realize the *purpose* of their learning. They *own* their learning."

The idea of teaching problem solving by learning to *use* tools, rather than just learning *about* them, is core to rewiring education. This is what the B means in my 21st Century ABCs of Learning: *build*. It's not enough to *tell* digital natives things; we need to let them *do* things. Students must be able to get their hands dirty and create, discover, and build things. This is what Musk understood, and it's why he pulled his own children out of one of the most prestigious schools in the country and made a new one designed around the idea of building to learn. What Musk really did, whether he refers to it as such or not, was move his children into the emerging world of the *Maker Movement*.

THE MAKER MOVEMENT

Dale Dougherty coined the word *maker* to describe people who, as simple as it may sound, like to make stuff—whether an engineer designing a new computer or a kid creating a functional piggy bank out of Lego blocks. "It's a fairly neutral term that could mean a lot of things," he said in an interview.[50] "I still like it for that purpose."

Not only did Dougherty give the movement its name, but he's also the primary person responsible for its rapid growth and popularity. In early 2005, Dougherty launched *Make*, the bimonthly magazine that included specific step-by-step guides on how to build things. The idea was to provide a consolidated source for the DIYers (Do-It-Yourselfers) where they could read about cool new things that could be made by hand. He envisioned it as a worthy supplement to the broader, news-based *Popular Mechanics*—more of a niche magazine that could fill in some gaps. He had no idea that it would launch a cultural and educational revolution. Multiple terms and phrases have since appeared that reflect various maker components, including *maker culture*, *makerspaces*, and the *Maker Movement*.

Maker culture refers to the collective desire and preference of people to create things. Students are no longer content with being told about things; they want to make them—to learn about them through hands-on experiences. The digital-native generation likes to take things apart, attempt to reassemble them, and figure out how to build new things from scratch. But there's a significant difference between today's makers and yesterday's DIYers: a greater desire to collaborate with one another. In maker culture, the physical spaces where people meet up to engage in hands-on learning by building their own machines, robots, gadgets, household items, and anything else of practical use are called *makerspaces*.

A makerspace can be anything from an entire building or an empty room to a small, dedicated section of a classroom. The size of the space doesn't matter; what's more important is what's done with it. One advantage of many makerspaces is that they often have things like 3D printers and other handy tools (digital or not) that makers likely don't have access to elsewhere. This is, of course, in addition to the main advantage makerspaces provide: the ability to collaborate in real time with other like-minded people. The classic DIY culture is gradually being replaced by a new DIWO (do it with others) culture, and it's this change that's driving the Maker Movement's recent popularity.

MAKER CULTURE

Living in this age also means that the sheer amount of information available makes it more difficult for individuals to stand out and differentiate themselves. Our psychological need for acceptance and recognition can easily go unfulfilled when there are millions of others around us doing the same things. The emergence of the maker culture is a direct response to this phenomenon, providing today's youth with clear opportunities for socialization, self-expression and creativity, and the chance to stand out from the crowd. Like all of us, digital natives desire autonomy—they want to be free to do the things they want to do, rather than just the things they're told to do. Maker culture empowers its members by increasing their sense of autonomy, which in turn increases their motivation to learn. It's why Elon Musk's children started to love attending school once they moved into a maker environment, where they could build the things they wanted to build and learn the things they needed to learn in order to build them.

Hobbyists have always tinkered away in their bedrooms, garages, and workshops, taking things apart and putting them back together again, either in their original form or an entirely new one. In the past, many of these people became the inventors that have provided modern society with everything we use, but they didn't have a lot of opportunities to collaborate or share ideas with others. It was this desire for sharing and collaboration that spurred Dougherty to launch *Make* magazine, its corresponding website, and a series of *Maker Faires*—modernized versions of the classic science fair.

It's my belief that the reason workshops and science fairs have remained small and niche for so long is because most people either have limited access to them, or are convinced that they aren't creative enough to become a part of such things. Many people claim they are not creative, but that's just not true. Steve Jobs explained it best: "Creativity is just connecting things. When you ask creative people how they did something, they feel a little guilty because they didn't really do it, they just saw something. It seemed obvious to them after a while. That's because they were able to connect experiences they've had and synthesize new things." Being a maker doesn't mean you must be naturally creative, just curious and willing to connect things.

Today, Dougherty's magazine, website, and Faires have become the primary places for makers to find new things to make and share the things they've already made, while making new friends and meeting new cocreators. Not long after the launch of the website, makers began arranging offline meetings, and before long both formal and informal spaces for makers began appearing in schools, libraries, museums, and universities.

Amazing things are being made in these spaces, too: robots, drones, motherboards, personal electronics, and more. With the advent of 3D printing, it's now possible to create almost anything. As a major *U.S. News & World Report* article reported, "In Texas, a 13-year old boy built a robot that could rescue victims of natural disasters. In Georgia, a 15-year-old girl developed a device that alerts parents who have left their child in the car. And in California, a 13-year-old boy created a Braille printer that would be almost six times cheaper than the currently available model."[51]

Whatever is being made, the one thing that all makers have in common is the willingness to move away from being passive users and to embrace their new roles as active creators—and the joy that comes along with that.

The current Maker Movement reminds me of the Homebrew Computer Club that Steve Wozniak, Steve Jobs, and other early hackers frequented in the late 1970s, where technology enthusiasts collaborated and competed to build the coolest new electronic devices. It's no coincidence that the entire personal computer industry was born out of these kinds of clubs. And that industry built the foundation of the world we now enjoy. If schools were more like *makerspaces* than *memorization races*—in other words, relevant, creative, challenging, and collaborative—our kids would have a much better chance of succeeding.

OPEN WORLDS

The popularity of the Maker Movement, and the culture that's driving it, offers us a good example of how it's basic human instinct to want to create things. It's why LEGO, Lincoln Logs, Silly Putty, and Etch-a-Sketch are some of the bestselling toys of all time, and why LEGO Mindstorms (LEGO-based robots that kids can program) are racing ahead today. At the root of this desire to make things is our broader psychological craving for autonomy, as we've seen, but that desire for autonomy itself stems from another deep desire of ours—freedom. Today, digital natives have become accustomed to having a great deal of freedom and choice in everything that they do—and one of the things they do a lot of is play games.

In prior generations, "open world" entertainment like the tabletop game *Dungeons & Dragons (D&D)* and the Choose Your Own Adventure books provided millions of kids and adults with unprecedented autonomy in an area—games—typically dominated by linear paths. In *D&D*, for example, players would embark on massive quests that required dozens of on-the-spot decisions, each of which would take the story in completely different directions. Because of this, no two *D&D* campaigns were ever alike, giving players access to an entirely new game experience each time they played.

As the home-based video game industry began to surpass the toy industry at the turn of the twenty-first century, titles like *EverQuest, World of Warcraft, Final Fantasy*, and *Grand Theft Auto* were set in massive open worlds in which players started the game by being dropped in the middle of some mysterious area with the ability to do almost anything they wanted. There were no rules, no set paths, and often no way to win, or even finish the game at all.

Many game developers at the time questioned the viability of these never-ending, no-win games, arguing that gamers needed rules, directions, and completion to be satisfied. Boy, were they wrong! To date, *Garry's Mod*, a "sandbox" physics game that relies heavily on user-created content, has sold 10 million copies; *World of Warcraft*, 14 million copies; and *Minecraft*, the mother of all open worlds where the entire goal is just to build stuff, and which has become the best-selling computer game of all time, over 26 million copies. It's also, across all platforms, the second-best-selling *game* of all time, selling a whopping 122 million copies![52] That's a whole lot of people who want to build stuff, and they're doing so not because they want to be "educated," but because they want to learn, discover, and create in a no-stress environment.

Digital natives are drawn to open worlds like the ones in video games, and it's critical to our ability to keep them motivated that our system meet them where they are. Consider one of the more popular types of games that they play today, the MMORPG, or *massively multiplayer online role-playing game*. The name alone tells us all we need to know about the difference between what the kids want versus what schools offer. "Massive" refers to the size of the game world, which directly relates to the amount of autonomy a player has by the simple fact that there's just so much more to do. "Multiplayer" refers to the collaboration that's so important today in the real world, but in many classrooms is referred to as *cheating*. "Online" refers to the use of the internet, which in most classrooms is being underused, misused, or not used at all. "Role-playing" refers to the ability of the gamer to become someone else, through a digital avatar, which points again to the player's need for autonomy and creativity. Last, "game" refers to play being fun and engaging.

Unfortunately, most schools shy away from an open-world model of learning, where autonomy takes center stage. As kids get older and make their way through our extremely structured system of education, they are invariably forced to push nonlinear thinking and creativity aside to focus instead on direct paths, which I view as a mistake. Instead of open worlds, education instead looks more like old-school games, with specific rules and linear paths for all. School books are not choose-your-own-path; they have chapters that must be read in a very specific order. School missions are not "find and explore" ones like those in MMORPGs; they're the kind of pattern memorization and repetitive motion that were needed to master out-of-fashion games like *Pac-Man* and *Donkey Kong*. The game being played in schools today is about *winning* (grades, test scores, etc.), rather than discovering, creating, and building—the things that kids both want and need. This is particularly ironic considering that *creativity* is the number one thing society associates with genius. As E. O. Wilson, the legendary biologist and author, once said about what matters most, "It is not IQ, it is creativity." What we value must begin to align with what we teach.

The aforementioned *Minecraft* is perhaps the most popular educational video game on the market today, yet it has never promoted itself as being an "educational" game. If it had, it would not have been able to reach its extraordinary level of success. Kids don't want to play educational games, no matter how fun they may be. It's becoming more and more clear that they would rather play a methodical, slightly entertaining mobile game like *Candy Crush*, than even the most fun and interesting "educational" or "learning" games. The reason is that words like "educational" and "learning," in their minds, imply *work* rather than *fun*, and not many people I know would prefer the former to the latter. If you want to create an *educational* or *learning* game that kids will *want* to play, then don't use the words *educational* or *learning* at all; just call it a *game*.

TO THE STARS

So, what have the results been of sending Elon Musk's kids to the Ad Astra "stars" rather than keeping them bound to the ground? "They really love going to school," he noted. "They actually think vacations are too long; they want to go back to school." Building things leads to the ultimate teaching tools—inspiration and motivation. It makes kids *want* to learn, and as I've established in chapter eight on Challenge-Based Learning (and throughout this entire book), I'm a big believer in not teaching kids by telling, but letting them learn by doing. I predict that the Maker Movement and interactive games will continue to become popular as digital natives continue to grow up demanding more autonomy and ways of expressing their creativity. Luckily for them, there's another large movement taking place right now that is offering them one of the best ways imaginable to achieving these goals, and it's being fueled by *coding*—the universal language of technology, and the final letter of my 21st Century ABCs of Learning.

CHAPTER 11

CODE

*Learning to write programs
stretches your mind, helps you think better,
and creates a way of thinking about things
that I think is helpful in all domains.*
—BILL GATES

’ve always had a fascination for computers and technology,”
said Thomas Suarez as he stood onstage, in front of the bright
lights and cameras, giving his first TED Talk in Manhattan
Beach, California. “And I made a few apps for the iPhone, iPod
Touch, and iPad.”

It was October 2011. Thomas wore a light blue, untucked
button-up dress shirt with khaki pants. He held an iPad in his left

hand that he used to control the large Keynote slides behind him. His talk was about the importance of giving kids the opportunity to learn how to create and develop apps. "A lot of kids these days like to play games," he noted, "but now they want to *make* them." He gave his 4½-minute speech, livestreamed for the world to see, with an air of confidence that typically comes with the credibility of a college professor or senior engineer.[53] Thomas was neither, but his own credibility was no less impressive. He knew what kids wanted, because he *was* one.

As twelve-year-old Thomas casually graced the stage and continued his speech, he talked about being inspired by Steve Jobs, and how he was able to use the iPhone's software development kit to help teach himself how to create apps. "I've started an App Club at my school that a teacher there is kindly sponsoring," he notes. "Any student there can come and learn how to design an app. This is so I can share my experience with others." I think this is a perfect example of everything discussed so far coming together: potential, motivation, learning, and digital natives' need to both create and share. It also brings us to the importance of the final piece of my 21st Century ABCs of Learning: *coding*.

Coding, a.k.a. computer programming, is the language of technology and, I believe, is one of the most important things that we should be teaching kids of all ages. I say this not because I expect all kids to become professional app developers like Thomas, but because the *process* of learning to code doesn't just benefit those interested in being programmers or engineers; it benefits everyone. I don't want to create a world filled with computer programmers, just one filled with people with the ability to *think* like them when it comes to solving problems. No matter what a child's learning style or intelligence type may be, the kind of critical thinking that is learned in coding is greatly beneficial.

BUT WHY CODING?

I see coding as an important skill to learn for several reasons, and when it comes to discussing why, I once again tend to start from the inside and work out. On a psychological level, learning to code has been shown to give kids a significant boost in self-confidence. Because coding is popularly seen as being difficult to learn and understand, even learning its most basic tenets can go a long way in helping us believe in our own capabilities and potential. I've seen kids with low self-esteem start turning things around after learning a single programming command, such as making a computer figure walk a straight line. Self-confidence leads to improved motivation and, as we've seen previously and as Thomas has kindly reinforced, a highly motivated student has the potential to learn and succeed at anything.

Aside from the psychological benefit of learning to code, it teaches tons of practical skills that have nothing to do with programming computers. For example, learning to code boosts both critical and computational thinking skills, just as some math can.[54] It also allows for the sense of creativity and autonomy that digital natives need. Most important, success in coding can translate to success in other areas. Kids don't need to learn how to code for the sake of coding; they need to learn how to code because the process of learning *how* to code is the same process that teaches them to think logically and visually and imparts other important lessons.

When we teach math to students, we don't do it with the express intent that they become mathematicians; we do it because we know that the process of learning math will help them *think* better. The same is true with coding. But although we may not expect students to become programmers when we teach them the coding skills that can make them better designers and creators, it does, in addition, give them a skill they can use to get high-paying jobs. In fact, computer science has become one of the highest-paid careers for college graduates, and computer programming jobs are growing at twice the national average[55]—yet only a handful of graduates are adequately prepared for these jobs after college. Whatever career a child who learns coding chooses, logic, algorithmic thinking, and problem-solving skills can all benefit them in that field.

Coding is just one aspect of computer science and has to do with the learning of programming languages like C++, Java, and Python. However, learning one language over another isn't nearly as important as learning the process itself. Specific languages will change over time, along with the technologies that rely on them, but the process of learning how computer language works, and how to use it, is foundational. I'm in no way suggesting that kids learn any specific computer programming language, but rather that they learn the process of learning them. Just as the research on CBL taught us, when it comes to learning, the process matters more than the product.

Not unlike the makerspace movement, coding brings together some of the most important things that digital natives need to know, including critical thinking, problem solving, and creativity. Society is finally beginning to realize just how important digital fluency is, as a full-blown coding movement is in full swing and spreading.

THE CODING MOVEMENT

As the TED Talk audience watched Thomas speak, many were surprised that a twelve-year-old kid could have learned to code so well that he's already designed and developed his own apps. But this isn't as uncommon today as one might assume. The idea of teaching computer skills to kids is far from new, dating at least as far back as the early 1960s when Alan Perlis, a respected computer scientist, gave a lecture at an MIT symposium titled "Computers and the World of the Future."[56] Perlis believed that everyone, including K–12 students, should learn to program as part of a basic education. Of course, there weren't personal computers at the time, and most students did not have access to the larger ones, so Perlis's ideas were way ahead of their time. As we've seen, it wasn't until the mid-1970s, when the Apple I and Apple II were released, that kids were able to get their hands on a computer, much less begin to learn how to program one.

Computers kept growing in availability and popularity for decades, but were still viewed mostly as a thing for "nerds" and "geeks." Coding seemed far too abstract for most people to make sense of, especially kids without anything relevant to compare it to.

Then, in 2005, Scratch, a free visual programming language, was developed by Mitchel Resnick at the MIT Media Lab. Unlike traditional coding, which appears as gibberish to those who aren't familiar with it, Scratch provided a visual language that allowed users to create their own games, interactive art, music, and animations. It showed people in a visual way what coding could do, and helped reduce the fear of learning to code; if languages like C++ and Java are hardcore drugs, Scratch is a gentler, ease-you-in gateway drug. Scratch gave kids the ability to understand programming logic and let them create and build things from "scratch." It made programming user-friendly, fun, and engaging. Before long, a large Scratch community arose online and began using the slogan "Imagine, Program, Share." Indeed, Scratch was founded as an open-source project with the idea of encouraging users to collaborate and share with others. (And today the platform has over 100 million users worldwide.)[57]

It wouldn't be until 2012, however, that the current K–12 coding movement really started to grow, as a program called CodeHS started specifically targeting teens by offering high schools access to their online curriculum and teacher tools. Simultaneously, for-profit "learn to code" boot camps like the General Assembly and nonprofit workshops like Girls Who Code also began popping up around the country.

Perhaps the biggest turning point in expanding the idea of teaching kids to code came in early 2013, when brothers Hadi and Ali Partovi decided they wanted to do more to help everyone (rather than just geeks) learn computer science. If Steve Jobs's vision was "to put a computer in every school," it was the Partovi brothers' vision to ensure that people didn't just understand how to *use* these things, but also how to *create* things with them.

To help spread their vision, the Partovi brothers created a video to promote the topic, called "What Most Schools Don't Teach," which quickly spread across the internet. Before long, principals and teachers from over 15,000 schools had contacted them for help. In response, the brothers launched a small website they called Code.org. Their mission was "to ensure that a quality computer science education is available to every child, not just a lucky few." The new website started receiving press and quickly found itself at the center of a new movement. Code.org soon grew and began expanding their services to include course design, teacher training, policy consulting, and marketing.

The same year that Code.org launched, Scratch 2 was released with a great deal of publicity. The following year, in 2014, came the release of the extremely popular iPad app ScratchJr, created specifically to teach five- to seven-year-olds the basics of coding. ScratchJr began taking off in education circles, mainly because people in the Scratch community began developing programs for it that could teach kids not just coding, but also math, history, photography, and dozens of other topics. Teachers were quickly finding that they were able to customize the program to meet their needs and began adopting it more and more.

Meanwhile, Code.org continued chugging full speed ahead to reach its vision. One of its most successful initiatives was a massive collaboration with other organizations and schools in what was referred to as the Hour of Code. The goal was to introduce programming into the school curriculum and raise awareness about the vast potential that comes with learning to code. To accomplish this, the Hour of Code was designed to teach the basics of computer programming through a set of sixty-minute tutorials that were both simple and fun. Think of it as a toe-in-the-water approach to introducing a subject that many people consider to be quite complex. Apparently it worked, because nearly 200 million students were exposed to coding during the 2016 Hour of Code event—which, not coincidentally, took place during another Code.org event, Computer Science Education Week.

Many of the major technology companies played a role in ensuring the Hour of Code's success, including Google, Facebook,

Microsoft, and Apple. At Apple, we offered free workshops inside of our Apple Stores that engaged resources from both Code.org and our Swift Playgrounds, and gave people the opportunity to host their own Hour of Code workshops. Both our participation in the Hour of Code and our rollout of Playgrounds became part of our broader "Everyone Can Code" initiative, in which Apple created a set of resources designed to help *everyone* learn to code regardless of age, background, or experience.

At Apple, I was especially proud of our rollout of Swift Playgrounds as a means of reaching and teaching kids. The software allowed kids to easily program drones and robots without knowing what coding is or even how it works. Through simple drag and drop, kids could easily see how simple commands communicated to a computer, tell the computer what to do—and then watch as it (hopefully) does it. If it doesn't, they could make adjustments until it does.

Rather than just showing kids a screen of cryptic code, Playgrounds also let them see what they were coding visually. For example, if a kid was learning to code angles on a lunar landing, they could actually see a visual representation of that lunar landing based on their code. This brought their code to life in real time, which made all the difference. The four types of Playgrounds were *Sphero Playgrounds*, where a robot ball can be guided through tricky obstacle courses; *Dash Playgrounds*, where kids could make a robot talk, sing, and respond to the environmental stimuli; *MeeBot Playgrounds*, where kids could make a robot dance and move in other lifelike ways; and *Parrot Playgrounds*, where flying parrot drones can be made to do acrobatic maneuvers in the air.[58]

Programs like Swift Playgrounds and ScratchJr, along with apps like Kodable, Tynker, and Pocket Code and initiatives like

Code.org's Hour of Code, Apple's Everyone Can Code, Microsoft's Make Computer Science Count, and Google's CS First, worked together to ensure that tens of millions of kids, parents, and teachers became more aware of coding's potential to make a difference in the lives of their children. One other key development, which has even more recently been quite impressive, has been the creation and success of LEGO Mindstorms, a programmable construction set system named after the influential book *Mindstorms: Children, Computers, and Powerful Ideas* by Seymour Papert.[59] Mindstorms lets kids turn a special version of something they already know and love (LEGO) into fully programmable robots.

Papert was codirector of the MIT Artificial Intelligence Laboratory from 1967 to 1981, and before that worked directly with legendary psychologist Jean Piaget, one of the key pioneers of self-directed learning and *constructivism* (where learners construct new knowledge from the interaction of their experiences with previous knowledge). It's no coincidence, then, that the importance of hands-on, inquiry-based learning discussed in previous chapters is fast becoming such a good fit for the potential use of technology in education. But as the public has become more aware of the coding movement's importance, the real question is: *What are we doing about it?*

CODING IN SCHOOL

"The very first Apple I that was ever built was actually given to a person back in the days before computers were ever even heard of," Steve Wozniak remembers, "who wheeled it in to a school and taught fourth through sixth graders a little bit of the elements of what a computer is." When Woz tells that story, I can't help but think this may very well have been the first time any students had ever seen a computer. Today you would have a difficult time finding any school without at least one. But having them and knowing how to create things on them are two different things.

While most people will agree that computer science and/or coding itself are valuable things for kids to know, there is less agreement on how to ensure they actually have the opportunity to learn it. Should it be the school's responsibility to teach it or parents'? Should it be optional, like electives, or mandated, like core subject areas? Should it be taught in high school, middle school, or elementary? Last, if it is implemented into the academic curriculum, what would it replace, considering there is only a limited amount of school time per day? These are difficult questions to answer, and states and school districts are still grappling to figure them out. For schools and districts that believe that computer science or coding should be a part of the academic curriculum, there still remains the big question of whether it should be mandatory or optional.

I have found that most people aren't fans of being told what to do, and this includes having things mandated or forced upon them. Even so, society as a whole has come to accept that certain academic subjects are so inherently important, or foundational, for students to learn that they should be required before they can graduate. In the United States this almost always consists of the big three subject areas: math, science, and reading. Beneath the big three is a second tier of subjects that are also more often than not "required," but are a lot less emphasized, and include things like history and social studies. In a tier below this lie subjects that at one time or another may have been considered important, but over time have become even less emphasized and, in some cases, even relegated to elective status. These include things like physical education, art, and music. Right now computer science, technology, and coding, for the most part, exist in this bottom tier. But should they?

In 2013, an Edutopia article headline asked, "Should Coding Be the New Foreign Language Requirement?"[60] I think that's a good question and the answer to it depends, once again, upon what we, as a society, view as the purpose of formal education. If we see education primarily as a means of career readiness, then an argument can be made that learning to code is actually *more* important than learning a foreign language. If we see the purpose of education as primarily being a means of teaching kids *how* to think, then again, there aren't many subjects that can do a better job of this—possibly more effectively than learning a foreign language can. Yet fluency in a foreign language is currently a high school graduation requirement in nearly all U.S. states. The Edutopia article suggests that we mandate foreign language instruction in high school "for reasons that relate to expanding communication abilities, furthering global awareness, and enhancing perspective-taking." But computer science can do all of these things and more, even as it's still seen more as an elective than a core subject. Some states, however, are beginning to see things differently. Texas recently passed legislation that enabled computer science to fulfill the high school foreign language requirement. I see this as a step in the right direction.

Some argue that computer science should be mandatory training in high school, and some ambitious cities, like Chicago, are actually experimenting with this. But I feel as though waiting for high school to introduce coding is far too late. Its foundational elements, as with math, should be taught as early as possible; some of the broader concepts should be introduced as early as kindergarten. These can also be integrated into other areas of learning throughout elementary and middle school, with optional ways of continuing on this path once a student reaches high school. In states like Virginia and Indiana, digital literacy has become a mandatory part of their state standards, a subject all K–8 students are expected to know. Because they learn the foundations of technology and coding in elementary and middle school, continuing into computer science in general, or even specific languages, once they enter high school becomes a legitimate option.

Research by the Education Commission of States shows that twenty-five states currently require their school districts to allow students to apply specific computer science courses toward completion of math, science, or foreign language requirements.[61] Eventually computer science, or at the very least digital literacy, will start being mandated in schools around the world, just as math and science are today. Whether it is taught as a separate subject, or as integrated parts of other subjects, there is just no way around the fact that it must be taught if we hope to thrive in the digital world we currently enjoy. For this to happen, though, we must be ready, willing, and able to help schools better understand *how* to teach it, as well as providing them with the resources needed to do so. Today, most schools don't even have a computer science teacher, and while Code.org and others have taken the lead in helping to train more of them, we still have a long way to go.

A few years ago, Apple ran an app-development experiment in Brazil. We provided technology to ten universities, and a hundred student volunteers at each learned to create mobile apps. There was no credit offered, just the opportunity to use technology and write iPhone apps. The CBL framework was used to teach the students, and their initial apps had to be in the App Store within two weeks, a second app by midterm, and a final app project at the end of the semester. What we learned along the way was that the process to write an app is very similar to the process of starting a company, so we adapted, and the coding classes became entrepreneurship classes. My education team at Apple also began working with our retail architects to design learning spaces based on Thornburg's model. The project turned out to be quite successful, with almost all of the students either getting jobs at tech companies or starting their own. The demand is real; we just have to get the supply up to meet it.

Thomas Suarez's best moment in his TED Talk, which has already been viewed over six million times, was when he went off script in a rare bit of improvisation. "These days students usually know a little bit more than teachers with the technology," he said spontaneously as the audience laughed in agreement. Realizing that what he had said didn't quite come out as he had hoped and unsure how to continue, Thomas smiled and paused for a moment. "So . . ." he said, then smiled and emphatically shrugged his shoulders, adding, "Um, *sorry*." It was the purest, most innocent moment of his entire talk, and it underscores just how far we still have to go to ensure that our teachers are prepared enough to meet the needs of today's students.

CHAPTER 12

TEACHING

*The role of the teacher is to create
the conditions for invention rather
than provide ready-made knowledge.*
—SEYMOUR PAPERT

I magine for a moment that you're a rock star. Not the musical kind, but a teacher rock star. You're a high school reading teacher, well-respected among your peers, and you absolutely love your job, in spite of having to teach thirty ninth graders at once. You've been doing this successfully for decades: not a single student of yours makes it through your class without showing *significant* improvement in their reading ability. You're especially proud of being able to motivate and help those kids who need it most. Just this year alone you've already managed to raise several of your students' reading abilities by *three* entire grade levels! You often wonder how they made it to the ninth grade in the first place, being so far behind, but nonetheless you're thrilled that you were able to pull off such a miracle.

Overall the school year seems like a total success—except for one little problem. Apparently, according to your class's test results, you have *failed*. Now you're flagged as an "underperforming teacher" and are at risk of being fired.

"What the heck just happened?" you wonder.

Well, prior to the school year, your school got a new principal who had recently learned that, compared to test scores produced by some other high schools in the district, state, and around the world, your school's students are behind—*losing* the race to the top. "This is an embarrassment," your principal proclaimed upon arrival, and hurriedly gave a new mandate designed to leave no child behind, starting immediately. To accomplish this, he adopted a comprehensive set of common "core" proficiencies that included hundreds of benchmarks for *all* students to rush toward.

For you, this meant that it didn't matter if your ninth graders were properly prepared in eighth grade or not. And their progress during the year was irrelevant. What mattered was whether they were able to hit those new benchmarks *on schedule*. To ensure this, you were instructed to use only the new, comprehensive curriculum (as opposed to last year's) that the principal deemed was better. The good news was that resources like computers, teacher assistants, and tutors were allowed and encouraged. The bad news was that you had to find a way to pay for them yourself—and you get paid a teacher's salary.

Toward the end of the school year, all of your students were tested for grade-level comprehension by being given the same test, which they needed to finish in the same amount of time. Any of your students who failed to perform at grade level, for whatever reason, would be held back, and you would be held fully responsible if that happened.

As outrageous as this scenario may seem, this is precisely what's happening to teachers today. They "fail" because all thirty of their students aren't able to meet some arbitrary benchmarks quickly enough. In this hypothetical, you failed because your students were not all reading on a ninth-grade level by the assigned test date. The ones you helped the most did not pass their ninth-grade standardized exam. When those students arrived in your class they were reading at a fifth-grade level, but by exam day you only managed to get them to an eighth-grade level, which just wasn't enough.

The same demands are put on teachers all across the country. For example, a study done within the Chicago school system not too long ago that looked at reading levels in a fifth-grade class found that one student was reading at an eighth-grade level and another, within that same class, was reading at a first-grade level. In fact, the study found that the students in that one class were reading at *six* different levels. Even if their teacher was a superstar, the number of hours that it would have taken to get all of those students up to grade level, while still providing challenging assignments for those at or above grade level, would be more than the number of hours that the teacher had available.

The goals and expectations of education are not aligned when it comes to teachers, administrators, and policymakers; because of this, everyone has a different idea of what teachers should be doing, how they should be doing it, and the exact time frames in which it should be done. The end result is that we are asking our teachers to perform miracles every week. It is impossible for teachers to meet the needs of each of their students within the number of hours in a week. I remember when Steve Jobs used to ask me to complete innovative projects in miraculous time frames, I would always say to him, "I believe in miracles, Steve. I just don't believe in scheduling them!"

STEVE WOZNIAK

Steve Wozniak, a.k.a. "Woz," is a historic figure in American business, most famous for starting Apple Computer with cofounder Steve Jobs. While Jobs may have become the more widely recognized of the two Steves, it was Woz who built the first Apple computer with his bare hands, which led to the launch of the company in 1976.[62] A year later, Woz designed and led a small team in the development of the Apple II computer, which, when combined with Jobs's marketing genius, set the course for Apple to become the iconic brand it is today.

Recently, in October 2017, Woz launched a new online educational platform called Woz U, offering coding and multiple IT programs to "expose digital engineering concepts to students to nudge them toward a possible tech-based career," as well as a Certified Educator program designed to "develop the teaching knowledge necessary to become a co-collaborator with students engaged in technology-driven, project-based learning."[63]

Woz U is far from Woz's first foray into education, however. In fact, he had two dreams as a child—to be an engineer was one, and the other was to *teach*. His engineering feats are now detailed in history books, but few people realize that he had also accomplished his other goal, too—Steve Wozniak was a teacher. "I wanted to be a teacher my whole life," he confessed during a recent interview. "So, I became one." For eight years, once a week, he taught fifth graders about technology and computers.

Woz's passion for kids is evident to anyone who knows him. When my coauthor Jason brought his ten-year-old son, Miles, over to my house during a dinner I was having with Woz and others, it didn't take long before Woz had ditched all of the adults and taken off with the boy to find a quiet place to chat. Within minutes he was teaching Miles secret math tricks and sharing inspiring stories of his own youth. The adults didn't get Woz back until it was time to go. However, when he's asked about his thoughts on teaching in more formal ways, Woz harbors mixed feelings.

On the one hand, Woz shares my belief about the inherent potential within every child, as well as the critical role of motivation. His rule of thumb when teaching was simple: *knowledge is less important than motivation*. "While it was important to teach knowledge," he said, "it was much more important to make the class fun so that my kids wanted to learn. Everything that I ever did that was great in life was something that I wanted to do."[64]

On the other hand, as much as Woz loves teaching, he isn't a very big fan of the operating system that dictates the way he was *supposed* to be teaching. "The problem is that, as a teacher, you're not often in charge of even your own textbook," Woz says. "Your principal just gives you your textbooks and asks for a contract ensuring that you'll do these pages on Monday, these on Tuesday, these on Wednesday, etc. And if students don't get it one day, maybe they had a big field trip or were busy talking, you aren't allowed to go back and redo it to ensure the material has been learned. The problem is in the system itself."

THE TEACHER'S DILEMMA

The hypothetical that started this chapter, along with Woz's story of being a teacher, highlights just how difficult it can be for a classroom teacher trying to operate in a buggy system riddled with design flaws. The theoretical fix itself is a simple one: we must be able to personalize learning for each and every student. In education, attempting to do this is referred to as *differentiation*. However, there's a big difference between theory and practice. Differentiation is one of the most difficult things for a teacher to do, and even more so when they have a lot of students to teach in a limited amount of time. While some students will be able to keep up with any particular lesson, many others won't, and then teachers are often forced to leave them behind. This is why we sometimes see students failing who we know to be smart and creative. "I didn't like the idea of grading and I wanted every student to be able to progress," Woz remembers. "But that's a lot easier with a small group of six, or even seventeen, students than it is with thirty. I discovered that large class size was the biggest detriment."

What ultimately drove Woz (and many others) out of institutionalized teaching is what I refer to as the "teacher's dilemma." Teachers are not given the resources to actually meet the needs of today's students, and yet unrealistic demands are placed on them. This constitutes one of the fundamental flaws in our educational operating system: no matter how good a teacher may be, they simply do not have the time, or the resources, needed to personalize learning for dozens of students at once.

Even the most experienced and gifted teachers struggle under the weight of ensuring so many students are able to learn. There simply are not enough hours in a week to find, prepare, and deploy the appropriate learning activities that will help every student overcome their own unique gaps and challenges. Because of this, educators are forced to teach to a nonexistent average, reluctantly turning to Tayloresque efficiency over effectiveness, which leads to losing students at both ends of the spectrum—those who underperform and those who overperform as well. There's an old adage that goes, "If you try to please everyone, you end up pleasing no one." As Dr. Todd Rose has shown in his work on the science of the individual, that's true in education as well: teaching to the average is akin to teaching to no one.

Rewiring education to solve the teacher's dilemma involves removing the unhealthy burdens placed on teachers using a combination of psychology and technology. Previously we touched on psychology and asked that we reconsider the way we think about students. *Who are they? What are they capable of? What can we do to help them?* We looked at ways to better motivate them and at specific things that could be done to improve their chances of success. But for us to truly meet the needs of students, we also must do everything we can to meet the needs of teachers. And as nearly every teacher tasked with trying to teach dozens of individuals the same material within the same time frame knows, this starts, as Woz noted, by tackling the problem of class size. But just how small *should* a class be? What *is* the ideal teacher-to-student ratio?

"One teacher per student," Woz says. In other words, to solve the teacher's dilemma we must reduce our expectations of what a single teacher can actually do, and work toward reaching a 1:1 teacher-to-student ratio. "Of course," Woz adds, "we will never be able to afford one *human* teacher per student."

BIG CHANGES

What Woz is referring to is the importance of technology as a means of helping us realistically reach the 1:1 teacher-to-student ratio. The good news is that technology has improved so dramatically, just over the course of the past decade, that it now has the potential to do just that. However, before we begin looking at the specific technologies to do this, it's important that we look at the bigger picture. Truly understanding anything only happens when it's put into proper context, and this includes the use of technology. In terms of rewiring education to solve the teacher's dilemma, the context needed is *change*. Technology has changed; through artificial intelligence, adaptive learning software, virtual and augmented reality, and more, it's now possible for us to begin designing and implementing the 1:1 personalized learning environments that will empower teachers to be successful.

Kids themselves have changed, too. Being a child today is not the same as being a child when many of us were growing up, and as we've seen, digital natives are very different from any other generation before. Not only are they different socially, due to technologies like the internet, mobile devices, and social networks, but also physically. Recall John Medina's work showing us that all brains are physically wired differently from one another. Kids also *do* things differently. We now live in a mobile, connected, and global world, no longer limited by physical spaces. Digital natives are always on the go, be it physically or virtually. They rarely stick to specific technologies (or jobs) for very long before moving on to the next one. From MySpace to Facebook to Twitter to Instagram to Snapchat, it's only a matter of time before digital natives get bored and move on to the next big thing. Remember email? While many adults still rely on it, digital natives rarely use it. As my young niece so gently reminded me at dinner the other night, "Only old people email!" It's true. If I send an email to one of my teenage grandchildren, I have to text or Snap them just to tell them to check their email. If we hope to reach and teach digital natives, we must be willing to adapt along with them.

The way success is viewed has changed as well. When a lot of us were growing up, success meant being able to land a prime job at a large company or factory, rise through its ranks, and then eventually retire from that same company and sit on the beach the rest of our lives. To most digital natives, however, the idea of remaining with one employer, doing one job, for their entire lives is not very appealing. As far as solving the teacher's dilemma goes, this means we must begin to rethink the way we envision each student's perceived success. Static grades and standardized test scores are not the answer. Instead, progress- and mastery-based assessments work better at judging a student's success at any given time. Growing up in a world of information overload, it's no longer about choosing and sticking with a single thing, but about experiencing many things over time. To accommodate this change, we must begin providing students with more options within the learning process. More options lead to more interest, which leads to more motivation, and ultimately more successes. Yes, "successes" *plural*. For digital natives, success seems more about the journey than the destination, so perhaps their education should be as well.

THE TEACHER'S ROLE

Another thing that has changed over the course of decades is the teacher's role, but not in a good way. Since the advent of Taylorism in American education, their role has changed from preparing students to succeed in life to preparing them to succeed on tests. Year after year, promising new teachers enter enthusiastically into the profession, eager to do what they're supposed to—help kids succeed—only to quickly realize, as Woz did, that the system isn't designed for that.

I take that back; we want kids to succeed, all right—on *tests*! It's no wonder that over half of all new teachers leave the field in the first five years, or that we have had a significant teacher shortage for decades.[65] More and more every year, the teacher's role has changed from one of delivering motivation to delivering miracles, and this change must be reversed. Remember, the ultimate goal of *all* teachers, including parents, should be to identify and nurture the passion and unique gifts that are inherent in every child, and this cannot be done by forcing them to teach to a test. We must stop viewing teachers as glorified tutors hired for test prep, and rewire the system to one designed to unlock their own potential as well.

Rewiring education means changing the role of teachers to no longer be about assigning textbook chapters to read, handing out worksheets of information to memorize, and relying on standardized tests to assess. Their role must be to help students recognize their natural talents, and move from being a conveyer of information to a facilitator of learning. Instead of relying on traditional teacher functions, the facilitator relies on things like asking open-ended questions, guiding students through open-ended activities, offering individualized feedback, ensuring that lessons are relevant and engaging, offering real-world and hypothetical examples, fostering collaboration and creativity, modeling the act of problem solving, and getting students actively involved in their own learning.

I can't help but recall that, back in college, it was the professors who always gave "open book" tests who were the most interesting. It's ironic that students often hear "open book" and assume a class is easier, because there's nothing to memorize. But what anyone who has ever taken a well-designed open book test knows is that these are the *hardest* types of tests. Doing well on them requires knowing what information you're looking for, where to look, and what it means within the context of the question. Then you have to develop an argument/answer that you can explain, and hope it makes sense! In a way, these types of tests are as much a tool for learning as they are for assessment. I have found a good general rule for testing is this: if Google, Wikipedia, or Siri can answer our students' questions, then we're asking the wrong questions. Let's stop giving kids premade questions and answers, and begin leading them through an adaptive process that allows them to discover the questions and answers themselves.

Teaching digital natives means understanding that they are *active* learners who want to be creators, rather than just consumers, of content. As we've seen, engaging them as creators can be accomplished through the use of inquiry-based learning frameworks, like challenge-based learning, but also through the use of things like physical and virtual simulations, student-based portfolios, exhibitions, field trips, guest speakers, and especially student input and participation. You may recall the section related to the importance of "student choice" in our previous chapter on motivation. Even broader than student choice is *student input*, one of the most powerful, yet often ignored, tools that teachers have.

One needs to look no further than Melissa Bartlett, the 2003 North Carolina Teacher of the Year and National Teacher of the Year finalist, to find a perfect example of what can be done to engage students through input. As Bartlett said in a profile of her, in my coauthor Jason's first book, *Conversations with America's Best Teachers,* "I use student input from the initial planning process all the way through to final grades.It has really been the key to my success as a teacher." [66]

She wasn't kidding. In Bartlett's language arts class, everything she did included student input and student ownership. From the first day of class, her students became involved in helping to create the rules of the class and the consequences for violating them. They were also involved in deciding what books and resources should be used to learn upcoming standards, and how to go about learning them—be it through *Jeopardy!*-like games or simulations, role-playing, or media creation. They wrote or collaborated on her lesson plans, helped design grading and assessment criteria, and remained thoroughly involved throughout the year. As a result, there was a significant increase in her students' self-confidence, motivation to learn, and, for what it's worth, their test scores and grades.

Last, effectively teaching today's students also means rejecting the idea that content expertise is the most important quality of a great teacher. This has never been truer than now, where content is only a click, tap, or swipe away. Digital natives do not necessarily need their teachers to be *content*-experts, but they do need them to be *context*-experts. The things that inspire digital natives the most are those that are put firmly into the context of their own lives. For them, *who* and *what* aren't enough. They want to understand *why*. "Why do I need to know this material? Why does it matter?" Thus, the teacher's new role must be to make lessons as relevant to the student's world as possible. This is the most powerful way of ensuring that students will actually *want* to learn and therefore remain engaged in their own learning. It is the teachers with *context* expertise who will be most valued going forward.

The concept of what makes a great teacher has changed over recent years, yet these changes are not because of technology; they're because of what technology has made possible. Everyone who had children growing up during those years when technology was creeping into our personal lives has their own stories of how the kids embraced this new world, in many cases before the adults around them had gotten up to speed. A child visiting my grandmother's house asked why her telephone "had a tail." And a niece of mine told her grandmother, "I love you, Grandma, but I can't spend the night until you get Wi-Fi." At the time, that little girl was all of four years old! Incidents like that may be laughable, but at the same time they are reminders of how different the kids are who grow up in today's technological world.

PLAYING IT OUT

You'll often hear me talk about the importance of making learning *relevant* for students. Doing so speaks to their sense of ownership, boosts their motivation, and helps teachers begin to unlock their true potential. But what does "making learning relevant" actually look like? How do we make lessons that aren't relevant *appear* to be relevant? What does technology have to do with it? In other words, how does this actually play out in the real world?

These are good questions, and my answer to all three of them is the same: by using technology to teach digital natives, you *are* making learning relevant. To engage today's students, the topic itself doesn't necessarily have to be made relevant; it could just be the way it's *delivered*. When done right, even the most boring of topics can be made fresh and exciting for digital natives. Shakespeare, for example, certainly does not rank very high as most of today's students' favorite reading material, but by using technology and making the learning process itself more relevant, engagement goes up.

Larry Reiff is a freshman humanities teacher at Roslyn High School in New York State about an hour's drive from Manhattan. He's been teaching Shakespeare for years, but not quite the way he does today: he has incorporated technology to make Shakespeare become personal and gripping for his students. Using technology throughout his lesson plans to introduce each new topic, he's able to build understanding and give students an opportunity to apply what they've learned in the way that works best for their individual learning styles.

For his Shakespeare lesson, Larry teaches *Romeo and Juliet*, using an edition from the Folger Shakespeare Library with no stage directions, so his students will focus on the story, the character relationships, and the emotions. The first step is to study the prologue and create a short movie. As they begin their study of the play itself, Larry has them read aloud, trying out different inflections. The youngsters begin to grasp how an actor can convey different meanings from a single line. He also encourages them to try out different sound effects and observe how that can change the emotional tone of a scene.

As several groups do their own versions, Larry has students bring together all of their work on staging, movement, voice inflection, and sound effects into an iMovie production of their selected scenes. Groups share their work with the rest of the class so everyone learns from the different interpretations of Shakespeare's language though lively in-class discussion.

Once they have understood the impact of stage direction and voice inflection in their own performances, Larry sets them to work on a new activity to build on their understanding of the play. He has them watch a scene from two movie versions of *Romeo and Juliet*: the 1968 film directed by Franco Zeffirelli and the 1996 Baz Luhrmann production. The students then discuss the differences between the two, leading not just to a better understanding of the text, but also an awareness of how different interpreters can shape the attitudes and emotions of viewers.[67]

In another approach, Larry presents a different kind of challenge: what if Juliet and Friar Laurence were messaging each other over Twitter to discuss their plan after Romeo has been banished from Verona? Having students use hashtags to communicate their understanding of what the characters are thinking and feeling, students can apply a modern-day communication tool that they love to use, and Larry can then assess how well they understand this 400-year-old drama.

It's difficult to grasp that today's new breed of teachers, like Larry Reiff, not only get their students to read assigned portions of classic literature, but that the kids find themselves enthusiastic, even exited, about the effort.

For instance, Larry describes one of his students, Julia, as a perfect example of one who thrives in the new environment. Traditional tests and essays are not her forte, but she is an incredibly creative young woman and can express her understanding of complicated material in remarkable ways. "Mr. Reiff told us this was going to be a technology-based course," Julia said. "That was intimidating. I didn't even know how to use a computer." Then they began studying *Romeo and Juliet* and the classwork included reenacting scenes from the play and working on a video project to create a movie trailer. "I felt like I became part of the story," Julia recalls. "The whole story just started coming to life for me."

When asked about Larry's class, TJ, another of his students, mentioned that in another class later on, they studied *A Tale of Two Cities*, using a challenge-based learning approach. "The experience with CBL helped me to understand better. I found myself bringing up things I would not have before CBL." The experience, he said, "most definitely changed my motivation to learn. I feel I take a more creative approach to learning, feel more open about sharing my opinions. It's so great to work with other people because you get ideas from them and you can help each other understand things one of you didn't understand," TJ says. "Doing projects that you had to think about and getting creative ideas working with others just made the class so much better. It was as if we were teaching other people what we are learning.

That was very, very fun." It's not often we find many high school students describing reading classic literature as "fun."

The striking impact in all of this is that the use of technology itself can make the learning of virtually *anything* more relevant for digital natives. Larry Reiff uses it as a means to engage students by bringing literature to life; the same can be done in other subjects perceived as either boring or difficult to learn, including history, math, and, yes, even coding.

TEACHERS AND TECHNOLOGY

As we begin reviewing the role that technology can play in re-wiring education, I want to take a moment to clarify a few important points. First, in the previous chapter we discussed the growing need for every student to learn computer science and coding, but ended by suggesting that we don't currently have enough trained teachers to accomplish this. Given the teachers' dilemma described in this chapter, it may seem like an antithetical suggestion to now add something *else*, like teaching coding, to their already impossible list of expectations! So, I want to be clear on how I foresee this happening, given the context. Ideally, elements of computer science (CS) would be integrated within various subject matters through-out elementary school, one CS course would be required in middle school, and *at least* a few CS *electives* (but ideally a set of courses) would be offered in high school. The minimum needed to make this happen would be a single CS expert at the district level to collabo-rate with and train elementary school teachers on how to integrate it with other subjects, and at least one CS teacher in middle and high schools. Access to the technology itself is becoming more and more affordable every year, with free open-source software options for almost anything now.

The second point of clarification I'd like to make comes in response to a fear that many teachers have of technology, whether spoken about or not—the fear of being replaced. The number one threat to jobs in the United States isn't immigration, but innovation. One of the most unfortunate byproducts of technology is, and has always been, workers who have been either unwilling or unable to grow along with the technological innovations of the time. That said, let me be very clear on this: great teaching cannot be replaced by technology. The only thing technology can do effectively in a classroom is supplement good teaching. The best technology on the planet doesn't even come close to being able to do the things that great teachers can do. There's a reason why we chose to start a book about educational technology with psychology: because the human touch is the magic formula that makes technology work. The goal of educational technology isn't to teach, but to empower teachers to be more effective and efficient. Even the best-designed artificial intelligence in the world will never have the one thing possessed by great teachers—heart.

Remember the Tin Man from *The Wizard of Oz*, who spent the entire story in search of a human heart? What happened to him? Every time a piece of the Tin Man got chopped off, it was simply replaced by another piece that fit the role. In technology that's called upgrading. But without a heart, the Tin Man eventually rusted away in the forest, which is where Dorothy found him. Dorothy had a good heart. The Tin Man joins her, along with other key allies, on a highly successful adventure. In our story, the Tin Man is technology. Dorothy is our teacher. Neither are effective substitutes for each other, but they do an excellent job of supplementing each other. Together they are better than they could ever be alone. While technology certainly has the *potential* to transform both education and students, it takes great teachers to actually unlock it.

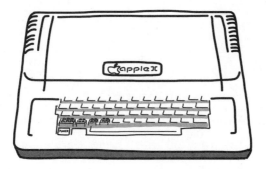

CHAPTER 13
TECHNOLOGY

Technology is only technology
to those born before the technology.
—ALAN KAY

I n 1978 my children attended St. Mary's, a K–8 school that
didn't have any computers at the time, so I worked it out with
one of the school's leaders, Sister Nicki, to let me donate a
couple of Apple II computers. It turned out that they didn't have
a clue what to do with these computers, as they were still quite
rare back then. Eventually, the school's faculty and staff cleaned
out the janitorial closet, put the Apple IIs in there, and announced
to the students that they could use them, but only during their

175

free time. One youngster, lagging badly in his ability to read, discovered a game on the computer that was designed to help kids improve their reading skills. Suddenly reading didn't feel like a struggle to him; instead, "it felt like a gripping challenge," he later noted. "Like a video game." By the time school let out for the summer, he had gotten himself up to his appropriate grade level in reading—by playing that game.

At the end of the school year the graduating eighth-grade class at St. Mary's raised the funds and bought additional Apple IIs for the incoming class, but that turned out to create a dilemma: there were now too many computers to fit in the closet! To solve this problem, they decided to make computers part of their standard curriculum, and one of the mothers, who worked for IBM at the time, was hired to be in charge of creating the course. Shortly after the curriculum was put in place, Sister Nicki showed me a copy of the first exam. The IBM mom had copied the front page of the computer manual and removed some words. The students were then asked to fill in the missing words. Suddenly, there were no more stories like that of the youngster who taught himself how to read better by playing a fun game.

By shutting the door on the janitor's closet and using the Apple IIs as little more than props for traditional learning, the IBM mom, without realizing it, had taken the joy of discovery out of the technology, replacing it with more of the same boring memorization tactics that the students saw day in and day out. All of the benefit that those Apple IIs brought when they were available for the kids to explore on had now vanished, and the learning took a hit. Seeing what happened at the time was a valuable lesson for me: discovering the incredible power that technology can bring to learning isn't always obvious. As I once wrote in an article titled

"How Apple Lost Its Way to School," "If we were not careful, our educational institutions will turn Steve Jobs' vision of the mental bicycle into an *exercise cycle*: something that's just boring and takes us nowhere."

The janitor's closet is a great story because it highlights the importance of understanding that adding technology to your school, classroom, or curriculum isn't going to do much in and of itself. What we ultimately do with that technology is just as important as choosing the right technologies to use in the first place. I see three key ways technology is implemented in the classroom: to make things more efficient, to make things slightly more effective, or to transform the learning experience altogether. Today, technology is primarily used as a means to solve problems related to the first two, but I don't think that's good enough. Relying on technology solely as a "tool" to make traditional processes more efficient underestimates its power.

All too often I hear the phrase "Technology is just a tool!" And while it's true that technology, especially *educational* technology, can be used as just a tool, that by no means is the only way that it can, or should, be used. To truly rewire education, we must raise the bar for technology. I made the case in chapter one that digital natives do not see technology as a tool at all, but rather as a natural part of their environment. However, many teachers and parents have yet to understand and/or embrace this. Take for example some of the most common ways we see technology being used in classrooms today: back-end software like databases, electronic grade sheets, wireless connectivity, internet browsing, and printing worksheets. These are perfect examples of technology being used to bolster efficiency—technology acting as a substitute for something that could be done just as well, if not as quickly, without it. While this can still be beneficial to a certain degree, it only scratches the surface of what's possible.

As educational historian and policy analyst Diane Ravitch said, "The virtue of a computer is that it requires a user, not a watcher." Technology has the potential to be transformative and motivational, and should be used these ways as well. It can inspire and motivate, inform and transform, better than almost anything else. It's time we start raising our expectations for educational technology and make it show us what it's really capable of doing!

MODELS THAT MATTER

To start the process of successfully incorporating technology into the classroom, it may be beneficial to at least be aware of a couple of frameworks that have been designed to help. While there are dozens of these related to educational technology, I'll only be touching on two of the more popular ones, as the reason that research models become popular at all is due to their being easy to understand, implement, or both. Keep in mind that frameworks are just that and are not meant to be followed every step of the way. Instead, I encourage you to learn more about them and then adapt them to fit your individual needs. I suggest treating all academic models as flexible suggestions rather than static directions. Even so, I still think they are worth knowing, as I'm a big believer in the idea that we should always try to learn the rules, before deciding to break them.

The first popular model that tech-savvy teachers often turn to when attempting to incorporate technology into their classroom is known as TCPK, originally created by prominent educational researcher Lee Schulman in the mid-1980s. Over time, as technology expanded into schools, later researchers built upon the model (and changed around some of the letters), and it is now sometimes referred to as "TPACK," with the "A" used to represent "and." Nonetheless, the original acronym stands for *Technology, Content, Pedagogy*, and *Knowledge*. This framework asserts that only when all four of these elements are in play can the most effective teaching and learning take place. In this framework, "Technology" refers to the physical resources used to teach, "Content" refers to knowing *what* to teach with the help of this technology, "Pedagogy" refers to figuring out *how* we can use the technology to reach the specific learning goals we're hoping for, and "Knowledge" refers to the know-how and skills that teachers need to effectively integrate each of these components.

TCPK was a response to researchers feeling that technology was too often being implemented without much (or any) forethought on how to use it correctly. "Thoughtful pedagogical uses of technology require the development of a complex, situated form of knowledge that we call Technological Pedagogical Content Knowledge (TCPK)," researchers Punya Mishra and Matthew Koehler announced at the time.[68] In other words, using a framework like TCPK gives teachers a way to ensure that all pieces of the technological puzzle are integrated with one another and serve a core purpose.

A second popular model for helping to define the role of technology in the classroom is SAMR, an acronym for Substitution, Augmentation, Modification, and Redefinition. This framework was developed by Dr. Ruben Puentedura when he was a consultant on the Maine Learning Initiative, a unique experiment conducted in 2002 in which Governor Angus King called for iBooks and laptops to be given to every teacher and student in the state. Rather than focusing on the proper use of classroom technology from a component perspective, as TCPK does, SAMR looks at it from the viewpoint of four individual *stages*.[69]

In the "Substitution" stage, technology acts as little more than a direct substitute for traditional tools, activities, and teaching. In the "Augmentation" stage, technology still acts as a substitute for traditional methods, but typically makes the old ways more efficient by adding other benefits for teachers and/or learners. In the "Modification" stage, significant elements of the classroom and teaching methods are modified to best suit the purpose of the specific technology, thus providing new opportunities for learning not available through traditional methods. It's within the Modification stage that the teaching and learning process starts becoming more effective rather than just more efficient. But the final stage, "Redefinition," is where the transformative experiences truly happen—where learning itself is, well, *redefined*. It's this final stage that provides the greatest opportunities for us to rewire education and meet the needs of our digital natives.

Since I know Apple's technology better than other technologies, allow me to use an Apple example to put SAMR in perspective. Assume you're a student wanting to write a book. If you use a laptop to type up your book in a word processor, rather than writing it by hand, that's an example of using technology in the Substitution stage. If you then use the Photos app on your iPhone to snap panoramic pictures of places and embed them into your book, this would be an example of using technology in the Augmentation stage. If you then decided that you wanted to collaborate with other students by using iBooks Author to cocreate an interactive book, you would be using technology in the Modification stage, because you are able to change the outcome of what it is you're doing, due specifically to these technologies. Last, if you decide to tap into the power of augmented reality and include immersive 3D holograms as a major component of your book, that would be an example of adopting technology from SAMR's Redefinition stage, because now you're redefining what's possible through the use of transformative new technologies.

These frameworks are just two of many options for integrating technology successfully in the classroom. I encourage you to dig a little deeper into these, and others, to experiment with the best parts of all of them, and then adapt as needed. This is the process that most tech-savvy teachers go through.

APPLE DISTINGUISHED EDUCATORS

The Apple Distinguished Educators (ADE) program[70] was created by Steve Jobs in 1994 as a way to highlight teachers who use innovative and exciting methods of integrating technology into the learning process. Steve was, as Tim Cook is today, extremely passionate about education, and both believe strongly in showing rather than telling. That's why the ADE program was created and maintained. It's a way to show teachers all over the world what's possible. We want to inspire and encourage teachers to think differently.

One of the things Apple did that has set the ADE program apart from other teacher-recognition programs was to design it to act as a kind of virtual "water cooler," as David Thornburg would call it. We wanted the best teachers in the world to talk among themselves: brainstorm, share ideas, and collaborate on better ways of doing things. What started out as little more than a small forum has now grown into the "ADE Community," a vibrant online (and offline) group with teachers worldwide actively sharing, comparing, and adding to best practices.

Apple Distinguished Educators also tend to go out of their way to share their work with the broader educational community, including other teachers, administrators, and policymakers. They are well-respected advisors to those of us inside Apple who are responsible for ensuring that the products and services the company creates are things that teachers both need and want.

Today, there are over two thousand Apple Distinguished Educators across the globe doing some amazing things, and their combined stories could fill an entire book all by themselves. I'm quite proud of what we've been able to accomplish with this program, if for no other reason than to be able to give these teachers a way to share how they have succeeded (and sometimes struggled) to better use technology. I encourage you to visit Apple's website where you can check out many of their profiles, read their stories, and even reach out to some of them for advice. I view the Apple Distinguished Educators program, and all of the teachers within it, as the epitome of what it means to rewire education.

TAKING IT HOME

One question I get asked a lot when teachers or schools are considering adding new technology to the classroom, especially iPads or MacBooks, is, "Should the kids take them home?" The concerns are the same: Will they get lost/stolen/damaged? What if they forget to bring them? What if they use the devices to get on the internet in inappropriate ways?

These are all legitimate concerns and my response is always, "It depends." All schools and classes are different and have different kids and cultures. There are technology-based solutions to some of these concerns, such as internet- and website-blocking software, protective cases, and built-in security programs such as Find My iPhone, but what it really comes down to is how much we trust our students. What I can say is that of all the teachers and principals that I know who have made the decision to let their students take devices home each day, none of them have ever regretted the decision.

A number of years ago, chemistry teacher Abdul Cohan took a big risk when offered the job of director at the Essa Academy, a school in his community of Bolton, UK, not far from Manchester. He understood it was going to be a challenge: the students mostly came from very poor families, more that 80 percent spoke English as a second language, and they were native speakers of an astounding twenty-six different languages. When he arrived, the school had an out-of-date laptop computer on an AV cart in each classroom, which was really only used to hold classroom doors open on hot days. One day, Abdul heard some parents in conversation, wondrously comparing notes about how much time their kids were spending on their cell phones—talking to each other, playing games, even looking things up for their schoolwork. And it struck him: if they are so adept with technology at home, maybe there was some way to use technology to help them learn better at school.

Rather than attempting to update the old laptops, Abdul raised the funds to purchase iPods, and later iPads, for each of his students. When a local newspaper heard that Abdul was going to let his students actually take the tablets home each night, it ridiculed the idea of giving devices to kids like this, warning that they would sell the units for pocket money. That didn't happen; rather, the students ended up taking better care of those tablets than they did with their own things.

After appropriate teacher training on the usefulness of the tablets and on tech-based learning, the tablets were given to each of Abdul's students. Suddenly, he remembers, "things at the school began to look up." This, of course, didn't happen overnight; the teachers had "a mixed response," he says. "Some jumped right in, some were very skeptical. We worked on creating a critical mass of people who understood the benefits."

What took place was a gradual transformation that eventually became what one newspaper at the time called "a remarkable shake-up in the way pupils are learning." Today, educators who visit the school are not so much impressed by the way the kids are using technology as by how *involved* they are in learning. And the transformation is reflected not just in the students but in the staff as well. Courses and textbook programs designed by the school's teachers have been downloaded in thirteen countries, a fact that Abdul describes as "a global presence" that generates "a very proud feeling" among teachers and students.

"In education," Abdul says, "we are very good at doing the wrong things really well." But it's clear that description does not apply to the Essa Academy. When Abdul arrived at the school, it faced closure because its students were performing so poorly: more than 70 percent were failing. Today, on the annual end-of-year national exams, every pupil in the school achieves the five "grade passes" that are the British measure of achieving the learning goals, and the school has been described as "a world leader in education technology." More to the point, the achievements at Essa offer compelling evidence of what is possible when determined parents, teachers, and school administrators are willing to set aside "how it has always been done" and replace it with "they did it, we can do it, too."[71]

One last takeaway that comes out of Abdul's story has to do with the pushback and ridicule that he received from the media about his decision. It's important to note that, if you're hoping to innovate or do things differently, you will always face backlash, and you must be prepared to push forward in spite of it. There are a lot of people out there who are no fans of innovation. After all, innovation is the *opposite* of tradition, and there are plenty of people who value tradition more. So, before we move on to looking at ways of implementing transformative technologies in your own classroom, I think it's important to take a moment to address some of the criticisms you will likely hear along the way.

THE BEIJING EXPERIMENT

In late 2016 an unusual research study on student potential was conducted in Beijing, China. Unlike other tests aimed at measuring potential, this one was conducted using a virtual reality (VR) headset, with all learning taking place inside of a 3D-world curriculum. Both the VR group and the control group had the same samplings of student performers (below average, average, and above average) and the same teacher. The researchers hoped to prove that learning in this environment would increase students' learning potential and performance, but what they actually found was completely unexpected. In a paper describing the study, the researchers noted that children who tested below average in the pretest examinations actually outperformed the pretest top scorers in test scores, learning comprehension, and knowledge retention. The average scores were 93% versus 73% for those who did not take the VR simulation.[72] "VR unleashes children's potential by letting them learn new concepts using the multi-modal model," one of the researchers said, "thereby enabling the brain to grasp new concepts in the way that's most natural to them."

When the tests were repeated a week later to test for retention, the margin of the blowout only increased, with the VR group averaging 90% and the control group dropping to 68%. "A dramatic change in actualized potential happened just by changing a single factor," the researcher said. These findings were interesting by themselves, but what made them *especially* interesting was the fact that almost exactly one year earlier, news reports from around the globe told a different story. "Computers DO NOT Improve Educational Results!" a BBC headline promised.[73] "Students Who Use Computers Often in School Often Have LOWER Test Scores!" a *U.S. News & World Report* article proclaimed.[74] So, what's going on here? How can some studies point to technology as a means of boosting student potential and performance, while others label it a factor in *lowering* potential and performance? Does technology help or not? To help solve this puzzle, let's take a look at a few key pieces.

MAKING HEADLINES

For starters, most of those headlines were based on recently reported data collected from a single research study conducted between 2009 and 2012. The study was done by the Organisation for Economic Co-operation and Development (OECD), the group responsible for administering the popular standardized test referred to as PISA, which tests fifteen-year-olds from dozens of countries on reading, math, and science, and is not very reliable.[75] This "study" was actually more of a poll, in which test takers self-reported answers about the time they spent using technology at school. OECD then compared the poll results to how each child scored on the actual PISA tests. What the comparisons showed was a correlation between the amount of time kids said they had spent on in-school computer use, and their scores on the actual PISA. Apparently, the more they used these computers, the lower their scores were. Some in the media latched onto this as supposed proof of the problems of technology and schools, with stories ranging from technology being a waste of taxpayer dollars, to suggesting that the only potential computers had in terms of education was the potential to *hurt* kids. Digging deeper into this research, however, suggests a different story, one that highlights frequent problems with testing the use of technology in education.

First, technology changes quickly. The difference in available technology from 2009 to 2015 is dramatic; there weren't many technologies around in 2009 that would be considered transformational by 2015 standards, much less by today's. During the years the OECD study polling took place, we mainly used computers to browse the web, view pictures, and send email. But what kids can do with a static website pales in comparison to what they can do and access with dynamic and interactive technologies like the VR used in the 2016 Beijing study.

A second problem with the OECD study is that its researchers focused on *if* technology was being used rather than *what* students actually did with it—exactly what I was referring to at the beginning of this chapter. Again, as with all technologies, how something is being used is just as important as what's being used. For example, consider prescription drugs. Just because a drug is proven safe and effective when used "as directed" doesn't mean you can ignore the directions and still expect them to work as advertised. Technology can be an enormous benefit to learning and creativity if it's used as *prescribed*—as a means to engage and motivate.

Last, the OECD study also uses a limited evaluation method— test scores on a single standardized test—that can conceal other measures of success. Most studies on student learning rely only on student test performance as the benchmark. If a technology is used and students' test scores go up, the technology must be good; if the scores go down or stay the same, then the technology must be essentially useless.[76] In contrast, the Beijing study looks at more than just comprehension. By retesting the same kids at a later date, they were able to measure the retention of concepts, and the process of critical thinking that led to the learning of those concepts—with dramatic results. What's becoming more and more clear is that these international tests are not very good measures of student success.

No matter what model you ultimately use as a starting point to integrate technology in your classroom (or home), be it TCPK, SAMR, or even your own framework, just make sure that you're using it to its fullest potential. The results of the Beijing experi- ment give us just a glimpse of what's possible when educational technology is used in ways designed to inspire, motivate, engage, and transform.

CHAPTER 14

TRANSFORMATIVE!

All books, learning materials,
and assessments should be digital
and interactive, tailored to each student
and providing feedback in real time.
—Steve Jobs

As technology continues to evolve, education must be prepared to evolve along with it, and we should continu-
ously raise our expectations for what it can do. And it's
capable of doing so much more than we're letting it. To change
this, let's stop viewing it as something that's working against us
and do what it takes to start making it work *for* us. And I don't just
mean in ways that make our lives easier as teachers and parents,

but also in ways that can completely transform the learning experience. Rewiring education is just as much about *how* a specific technology is being used as it is about *what* technology is being used. For example, an iPad, in and of itself, may not seem very transformative, but using it in certain ways can motivate, engage, and jumpstart extraordinary amounts of creativity and learning. So, which transformative technologies have the most potential to rewire education? Here are some of the most promising.

ARTIFICIAL INTELLIGENCE

Artificial intelligence, commonly referred to as AI, is of utmost importance due to its ability to personalize the user experiences of *other* technologies. As personalization is the key to effective learning, it makes sense then to begin our look at transformative *educational* technology with a brief look at AI.

Artificial intelligence is computer software with the ability to do things that can typically only be done through human intelligence, such as problem solving, decision making, and complex voice and visual translations. In short, AIs are computers that think like people. Because of the advancements made in what's referred to as *machine learning*, AI now has the ability to *analyze* so-called big data, *learn* from patterns that it finds within that data, and then *adapt* the way it thinks about things based on this new information—all without human intervention.

If there's one technology with *unlimited* potential, it's AI, because as computers begin to learn, think, and adapt by themselves, there really will be no more ceiling on possibility. Many high-profile people in the tech industry, like Facebook CEO Mark Zuckerberg, are extremely passionate about the possibilities that AI provides, while others, like Tesla and SpaceX CEO Elon Musk, are terrified of what AI could become, going so far as to warn about the danger of it being *so* ridiculously powerful that it's one of the biggest threats to the human race. The 2001 sci-fi film *A.I. Artificial Intelligence*, and the 2004 film *I, Robot*, starring Will Smith, both went a long way toward painting this darker look at what AI might one day become, but for now anyway, AI is helping to boost educational technology in extraordinary ways. Rather than delving into how AI works, I think it would more beneficial to explain AI by taking a look at other transformative technologies that AI makes possible.

ADAPTIVE LEARNING

Adaptive learning refers to software that uses AI to change the difficulty level of content being taught, automatically and in real time, based on previous answers and actions made by its users (i.e., the learner). One benefit is that adaptive learning prevents students from moving on to more difficult lessons before mastering current, simpler ones. This is especially helpful in subject areas like math and science, where each thing being taught depends on the learner's knowledge of and familiarity with something that was previously taught. For example, it would be nearly impossible for a student to get the correct answer on math *order of operations* lessons that include exponents and fractions, if the student does not yet have a firm grasp of how exponents and/or fractions work.

In a traditional lesson, given via worksheets or even on a computer, this student would simply get all of the questions wrong. But that doesn't help us, as that student's teacher or parent, figure out why he's messing up and, more specifically, where the actual problem is. Is it because he doesn't understand the idea behind the order of operations, or because of his trouble with fractions, exponents, or something else?

Of course, good teachers can still figure this out by having the student show all of his work and then going through it all step by step until the problem area is found, but what then? Usually at this point the class has moved on to the next lesson and he's already behind. I say, "he" as if it's just one student, but in reality, this teacher likely has over twenty students in that class, each lagging in some area or another, leaving an intricate and very large puzzle for the teacher to figure out—and quickly.

Not only that, but even if this teacher does manage to perform this requested miracle and pinpoint twenty-plus problem areas, again I ask—what then? That's the difficulty of classroom *differentiation*, and it's where adaptive learning software shines, because had it been used in this scenario, it could have done a lot of the "grunt work" such as figuring out specific problem areas for all twenty-plus students, within seconds, saving the teacher valuable time and energy that could better be used *teaching*.

Adaptive learning software forces students to work at their own pace, which is good, because it lessens the pressure they face to understand things within given time frames. If you recall from chapter five, on learning, this is one of the biggest problems that we face—students can learn just about anything, just not necessarily in the same ways, and certainly not within the same time frames.

Adaptive learning has also been shown to virtually eliminate cheating, because students are at different places in the lesson at different times, and to boost student confidence, often through built-in *gamification* devices like points, levels, and badges. While we have not been able to truly personalize learning for all students yet, I'm sure that adaptive learning technology will play a role in our finally doing so.

INTELLIGENT ASSISTANTS

Another transformative technology empowered by AI is *intelligent personal assistants* like Apple's Siri, Amazon's Alexa, and Microsoft's Cortana. Voice-activated machines and computers use natural-language user interfaces to recognize what's said when someone speaks to them. But what sets them apart from other things that do this, such as transcription software, is what happens *after* the program recognizes what's said. The AI running these doesn't just recognize what you *say*, but also what information you actually *want*, and gets it for you within seconds. Remember what we would have to do in the "old days" when we had a question about something? We would have to get our computers or smartphones, open a browser, type in the question we want, browse through the search results, and then read what we hope is a good answer to our question. Okay, this is *still* the most common method of finding answers, but that's changing as intelligent personal assistants are getting exceedingly "smarter" and gaining in popularity.

In using this type of technology, you would verbally ask your "assistant" (either in the form of a small box or mobile device) a question and almost immediately get an answer. For example, picture a student interested in space as he observes the night sky. He has a million questions about what he's looking at, but he isn't about to stop looking in order to whip his phone out and search for answers. Instead, let's say he's wearing a Siri-enabled smart watch and, while still looking up at the sky, says, "Hey, Siri." This alerts his watch that he's talking to *it* rather than someone else, which prepares it for a forthcoming question or command.

"How far away is the moon from Earth?" the kid asks. In seconds Siri responds, "The distance from the Earth to the moon is about 237,248 miles." The AI that runs Siri has listened to his question, translated it from voice to computer language, figured out what he actually wants, searched the internet for the answer, figured out the most helpful way to phrase that answer, and then verbally gives the answer—all in seconds! The student is then free to ask Siri follow-up questions, tell it to actually do something with that answer (i.e., make a note of it, save it, email it, etc.), or move on to another question altogether. Intelligent personal assistants are like having an expert on *everything*, following you around wherever you go, quietly awaiting your questions.

This kind of 24/7 access to instant information is why memorizing facts has become nearly useless. How could we possibly justify a student wasting limited short-term memory space holding facts that can be answered in seconds, when that same mental space could be better used for critical thinking? Intelligent assistants aren't just the future of information retrieval; they're already here, quietly awaiting your next question.

THE INTERNET OF THINGS

The Internet of Things (IoT) refers to technology like integrated circuits, electronics, sensors, software, and so forth that's embedded directly into common everyday items like clothes, appliances, cars, furniture, utensils, and just about everything else. IoT is typically connected directly to the internet, via Wi-Fi, or to other devices via Bluetooth. You might think of it like this: whereas intelligent personal assistants provide *content* information through devices, the internet of things provides information in *context*, intelligently communicated directly with the item's owner.

So, what might an IoT educational experience look like? For starters, by using radio-frequency identification (RFID) technology embedded into a student's ID or wearable device, for example, a teacher can easily track attendance without wasting time calling roll, and parents can know whether or not their child is even at school.

While reading her history book, a student could use a digital highlighter (which already exists) that wirelessly transfers the text she highlights into an app on her phone, making it editable and searchable and storing it in the cloud so that she can access it anywhere, anytime. Students could also offer to wear IoT-enabled headbands with built-in EEG sensors that can monitor cognitive abilities (which exist too) while they're engaged in specific lessons, giving their teacher real-time feedback on which activities increase student engagement and which don't, while also allowing easy identification of each student's preferred learning style.

Most important, real-time information given to teachers by IoT-enabled devices can allow them to more easily personalize the type of content needed to engage specific students, as well as the best way to deliver that content to them. They could then instantly determine which students may need the most help and proactively reach out to them, eliminating the need for students to have to ask for help, which for many can be embarrassing.

In 2016, it was reported that there are already over seventeen billion devices connected to the Internet of Things, with over thirty billion more expected to be connected by 2020.[77] Considering the IoT didn't really exist before a few years ago, I'd say these growth numbers give us a pretty good indication that it's not going away anytime soon, and it's only a matter of time before it becomes more mainstream in schools around the world.

MOBILE TECHNOLOGY

Right up there with the creation of the personal computer and the advent of the internet, there aren't many modern-day technologies that have transformed our daily lives more than mobile. From early PDAs, to cell phones, to smartphones, tablets, and now wearables, the evolution of mobile technology and the apps that drive it have been nothing short of miraculous. Smartphones, tablets, and wearables are quickly replacing desktop and laptop computers as our primary technological devices. Their small size and ultra-portability have allowed us to bring entire computers along with us wherever we go, and because we are always online, we can quickly tap into the power of the internet whenever we want.

What really makes mobile technology shine, especially in the world of education, is that they aren't just one-dimensional devices, like traditional TVs and radios. Rather, they're *platforms*—systems designed to *host* a variety of user-generated content and services. Smartphones, tablets, and wearables run on software platforms like Apple's iOS and Google's Android, just as Macs run on the macOS operating system and PCs run on Microsoft Windows. But rather than using traditional software like that found on old floppy disks, SD drives, and CD-ROMs, mobile device platforms are powered by (mostly third-party) "apps" in giant digital *ecosystems*. I remember, shortly after the iPhone's release, seeing a TV ad saying, "There's an app for that!" when referring to a problem that needed solving. Today, there are over two million collective apps in both major app stores (Apple and Google), with hundreds more being added daily. So, yes, if you have a problem, there's a very good chance that there's an app for it! I see digital platforms and ecosystems as continuing to be the future of mobile technology into the foreseeable future, although what form these will take twenty years from now remains to be seen.

So, what exactly is it that we're accessing, when we pull out our phones and fire up those apps? More and more, access to free content. Already most content is free and I believe that, eventually, nearly all of it will be freely available to anyone who wants it. This change has already disrupted learning and is gradually doing the same to formal education. Students access premium content through services like Khan Academy and iTunes U for free every day, wherever they happen to be, and schools across the country are registering accounts for all of their students in droves. Now that digital natives are getting older and apps are getting incredibly easy to design and create (thanks to things like Swift Playgrounds and Xcode), I think user-generated content will continue to grow at unprecedented levels.

The growing availability and affordability of mobile access, especially via tablets, has also boosted the activity of Web 2.0 sites and services like Wikipedia and Reddit, which are being powered by things like crowdsourcing (where people work together online to edit documents or solve problems) and cocreation (where people work together to design and create specific projects). Collaborative editing, via free software like Apple's iWork and Google Docs, and sharing, via social media services like Facebook and Twitter, are exploding in popularity.

The collaborative phenomena have grown beyond just being online too, as an entirely new type of economy known as the sharing economy has emerged, led by innovative organizations like car-sharing start-up Uber and house-sharing start-up Airbnb. The sharing economy, made possible through mobile technology, has taken the world by storm. While our world may at times appear to be getting more divisive, mobile technology, and the sharing economy that has spawned from it, is playing one of the biggest roles in helping to bring us back together.

3D PRINTING

One of the most exciting educational technologies, with the potential to completely transform learning, is the 3D printer. These machines, often not much bigger than a traditional printer, allow students to turn any digital file into three-dimensional physical objects. To me, this will be a real game changer, allowing students to print real, physical manifestations of just about anything. 3D printers can use a wide range of materials, and can make anything from a tiny model figurine to an entire house that can be lived in. In medicine, 3D printing is even being used to print human-like organs that, scientists believe, will one day eliminate the need for organ donors.

I view 3D printing as one of the best of the emerging technologies due to its clear relation to hands-on learning. Not long ago I saw a science school make particularly good use of makerspace in the form of a 3D printing lab. Some of the older students would take some of the younger ones with them into the lab when they were learning about volume. In the lab, the students 3D printed the first letter of each of their names as containers and then compared whose letter contained the biggest volume. It made the lesson more personal and the kids loved it. Rather than reading about volume in a textbook or memorizing a formula, the students were creating physical vessels in fun and exciting ways. What was most interesting to me was that the lesson involved students helping other students to learn without the oversight of a teacher.

Similar 3D printing labs are now popping up in museums and schools, where students can move ideas from concept to prototype quickly, converting the students from passive consumers to active creators. Science, history, and the arts are benefiting by allowing students to experience creative, hands-on learning, and teachers are enjoying the attention-grabbing visual aids that 3D printing produces. It's one thing to read about something; it's another to physically hold it.

INTERACTIVE BOOKS

There's a big difference between a traditional textbook and a digital, interactive one: the former are static, whereas the latter are dynamic. Note that when I say "digital, interactive textbook," I'm not just talking about an eBook. Just because an eBook is electronic doesn't mean it's any better or more innovative than a regular one. Often, eBooks are as static as a paper textbook, though they are more efficient, because readers can carry hundreds of them around with them at once! Interactive books, on the other hand, aren't just designed to make reading more efficient; they *transform* the reading experience itself by incorporating links, video, audio, crowd-based annotations, peer-to-peer sharing, and more. This kind of technology can provide memorable learning experiences far beyond any textbook.

Interactive books and textbooks are just now starting to live up to their twenty-first-century potential. The last big changes in books was the emergence of audio and electronic books, but while novel, neither was transformational and neither achieved widespread adoption in schools. I believe that this is because neither improved the experience of reading; they simply transferred the traditional book to a different medium. However, today we are seeing truly interactive books. 3D animations of images and videos literally pop off the page, giving readers multidimensional examples and tutorials of the concepts being discussed. Readers can access crowd-based annotations that use real-time collaboration software to translate the meaning of difficult concepts, taking the reading experience to levels we've only dreamed of in the past.

Apple's eBook application, iBooks, is an example of a platform where all kinds of digital books are hosted. Many of the most creative and interactive books on it were made by iBooks Author—in my opinion one of the most powerful tools around for creating next-generation books. iBooks Author has become one of Apple's most sought-after educational products, because now kids can do more than just learn how to read a book; they can learn how to create their very own, fully interactive books.

LEARNING TO SCALE

All of the technologies mentioned in this chapter have the potential to transform the educational landscape in different ways. All of them are already beginning to make an impact on smaller levels, making the real challenge one more along the lines of how to increase the access of them, or *scale* them, so that all students and teachers have the opportunity to benefit from them rather than just a lucky few. Scaling things that we *know* to work is in fact one of the most difficult parts of rewiring education.

Rarely has a technology, no matter how transformative it may have been, just popped up out of nowhere, quickly proved to the world that it works, and then instantly had half of that world using it. Slow and steady growth has been the rule. This is how most technology has scaled in the past, including the personal computer and almost every other transformative technology that exists today.

Remember those intelligent personal assistants I talked about, like Siri? Well, in 1987 Apple released a concept video of what we called the "Knowledge Navigator," essentially a *very* early prototype of intelligent personal assistants.[78] Today, looking back at the popular five-minute video dramatization of it, starring the lovable Bill Nye the Science Guy, I find it uncanny how much of the technology we actually got right—and it only took *thirty years* to get there!

The good news today is that the speed at which things that work are being widely adopted is starting to change. The reason is that information on what works and what doesn't is more readily accessible now, and social media and social networks, both transformative technologies as well, have allowed people to more easily communicate and share with one another. Today, things that work well tend to be able to raise enough funding, through donations or investment, to help them scale much faster than before. The length of time it takes technology to scale is changing for the better. Consider how long it took these products and services to reach one billion users.[79] Notice how much quicker it's getting:

1985: Microsoft Windows—25 years
1990: Microsoft Office—21 years
1998: Google Search—12 years
2004: Facebook—8 years
2008: WhatsApp—6 years

As you can see, the time it takes key technologies to be *able* to scale is significantly decreasing. The speed of the internet and the advent of social media have allowed information to pass between people at lightning speed. People are finding out about things that solve their problems faster, and when things actually do solve those problems, they tend to spread faster. This doesn't mean that *every* technology will scale, but it's a very good reason to be optimistic about the potential for transformative educational technologies to reach more kids, faster than ever. And it's a good thing too, because the technology with the most transformative potential, *augmented reality*, is already here, and if we can get it quickly enough to the millions of students that can benefit from it, it could change the future of education as we know it.

CHAPTER 15

FUTURISTIC

*Times and conditions change
so rapidly that we must keep our
aim constantly focused on the future.*
—WALT DISNEY

n the summer of 2016, I rarely left my house without seeing a group of people walking around randomly in packs, looking down at their phones. Often they'd stop, back up, and point excitedly at nothing in particular. Then they would exchange high-fives and strike up conversations with one another even though they were often complete strangers. This was my informal introduction to the mobile-based augmented reality game, *Pokémon Go*.

It was amazing to me that all these kids had gotten off the couches and embraced the outdoors, all in an effort to find and catch little digital monsters called Pokémon.

Being in the tech industry, I knew of augmented reality (AR), but what I didn't know was just how powerful a tool it could be for motivating people to go into the real world and *do stuff*. I witnessed, with my own eyes, teenagers *voluntarily* going into libraries and museums! Of course, I live in Silicon Valley, where kids do all sorts of strange things. I wondered: How many people are playing this elsewhere? Well, a lot, as it turns out. The *Pokémon Go* app set the record for most downloads *ever* in our App Store—and it did this in its *first week*! Within two weeks of its launch it had amassed over twenty million active users (more than Twitter), becoming the largest mobile game in U.S. history. *Pokémon Go*'s historic explosion of players first showed me the true potential of AR, not for games, but as a *motivational* tool. I knew the implications of this for education were enormous and I believed then, as I do now, that augmented reality will very soon play a *significant* role in what that future looks like.

AUGMENTED REALITY

Augmented reality overlays computer-generated content right smack onto our *real* world. In *Pokémon Go*, for example, small representations of "Pokémon" appear on players' phone screens as they move through the physical world, based on GPS signals, and players tap the creature on the screen to capture it. The AR part comes when you tap a button that turns your camera on and allows you to see the Pokémon superimposed onto the real world.

Whatever you're looking at through your phone's camera (your friends, church steps, a library shelf) will appear to include that Pokémon.

Virtual reality, augmented reality, and now *mixed reality* (MR) are all part of a broader field called immersive technology, also known as *immersion*. Since most people are more familiar with the idea of virtual reality than they are augmented reality, I have found that the simplest way to explain the difference between the two is this: VR uses headsets to place us inside of digital worlds, whereas AR brings the digital world to our physical world, and MR is a combination of both.

When it comes to VR, we have already seen some of the success it can have just based on the Beijing experiment results discussed in chapter thirteen. VR's 360° computer-generated environments are fully immersive 3D worlds that, hopefully, will one day enable teachers and students to go on virtual fieldtrips anywhere in the world, in the past, present, or future. Rather than the teacher bringing a *T. rex* into our world, as in AR, kids would be transported, via goggles, glasses, or headsets, to the *T. rex*'s world, where both it and its natural environment could then be studied. The long-term potential of VR is strong. I like the idea of giving students their own personal time machine, where just by wearing a headset they can go back eighty million years to the Cretaceous Period to walk among full-scale dinosaurs in photographic-quality 3D. Leading the way in this field are Facebook, with its Oculus Rift; Microsoft, with its HoloLens; and Google, with both Google Cardboard and Daydream headsets. Apple has been doing research and development in VR for years, but they are much more excited about AR.[80]

While the future of VR may indeed be bright, I'm personally and firmly in the AR camp for now, for two primary reasons. First, I'm not a big fan of kids completely disappearing into virtual 3D worlds. While it's actually very cool to experience VR in short bursts, we all know that these things (especially games, which *always* come first) will be highly addictive, and we may end up never seeing our kids again! I'm only slightly joking, of course. The second, more practical reason is because of what's quickly becoming possible for students, not tomorrow, but today. Rewiring education is not about predicting the potential of students and technology in some hypothetical future; it's about unlocking all of this potential today.

One of the most impressive schools I have visited, in terms of its ability to properly utilize technologies like augmented reality, is the Varmond School in Morelia, Mexico. Run by the school's founders, Noel and Noemi Trainor, Varmond is a PK–8 school built from the ground up to integrate technology throughout every aspect of its curriculum. Set within an adaptive, challenge-based learning structure, Varmond uses augmented reality, and other cutting-edge technology, in most of its classes. It has a 3D maker lab, interactive books, and mobile devices for all teachers and students. And every one of the learning spaces highlighted in chapter six is seamlessly integrated throughout the school. In fact, of the thousands of schools that I've visited in my career, I have never seen one that has successfully integrated transformative technologies, plus just about every other best practice, as well as Varmond. In many ways, the school of the future is already here and has been one of the best kept secrets in education.[81]

THE RISE OF A PLATFORM

Over the past decade, several organizations have made good use of AR at every level of education. One of the most pioneering of these has been the nonprofit television network **PBS**. As far back as 2010, PBS Kids launched an online AR game called *Dinosaur Train Hatching Party*, where kids had to traverse a combination of real and virtual worlds to help hatch a dinosaur egg. A year later, PBS Kids launched one of the first multiplayer, augmented reality 3D game apps, called *Fetch! Lunch Rush*, in which kids had to try to keep up with the lunch orders of a cartoon dog's movie crew. According to a press release at the time, the game "opens a new world of learning by teaching kids ages six to eight math skills, like addition and subtraction, while blending the virtual and real world into a truly engaging experience." The game fit perfectly into PBS Kids' goal for the technology. "Our goal is to use media to nurture kids' natural curiosity," said a PBS Kids senior vice president at the time, "and inspire them to explore the world around them."[82]

Another early innovator in the AR educational space was NASA, which in 2012 released its own AR app, *Spacecraft 3D*, where students could use their mobile phones to view 3D renderings of several NASA spacecraft right in front of their faces. These are just a few of the pioneering efforts in a field that is very much emerging. Since those early days, AR has quietly grown into a powerful, if still somewhat unknown, technology. More recently, however, things are *really* picking up.

In 2017, almost exactly one year after the initial *Pokémon Go* craze hit, Apple announced the launch of a new iOS-based AR developers kit, called the ARKit, which allows third-party iPhone and iPad app developers to easily incorporate augmented reality inside their apps.[83] This means not just Pokémon will be able to "appear" in your house or classroom anymore, but anything can. The options are virtually unlimited and include images, data, charts, graphs—you name it. Now we can position virtually *any* of these objects to look like they are actually being placed in real-world spaces. I don't mean just hovering over the space either, I mean *in* spaces. Because of an embedded technology called SLAM (simultaneous localization and mapping) and depth-sensing cameras, putting virtual things into real-world spots comes down to inches.

One of the best things about AR, from an educational standpoint, is that it can superimpose much more than just holographic images. It can also project maps, graphs, videos, and text, such as fun facts, definitions, statistics, and online comments. On a mobile device, these holographic projections can be triggered by using the device to view or scan an image or QR code, or upon arrival to a certain location, through *geotagging*. There are many other ways of seeing these holograms, too—through an AR headset, a digital camera, or a computer monitor. In each case, the device imprints the images on the lenses, in digital layers that can be added or removed by the user on demand. Through AR, all types of static content can be brought to life, from the periodic table, to biographies, to space exploration.

So, what can this do for students? Let's take a look at one scenario, where everything discussed is possible now, or will be within the next year or two. Remember the boy we met earlier who loved space and used Siri to instantly answer his questions? What's he supposed to look at and study in the daytime when you can't see most stars? Well, now he has a solution. All he would have to do is turn off the lights in his living room, launch a solar system AR app on his iPhone or iPad, and watch as the solar system emerges over his own furniture. As he then walks through his living room, comparing galaxy formations being projected in 3D by the app, he can also zoom in and out of these galaxies, in order to take a closer look at a specific star or planet, and use his finger to actually manipulate them, turn them around, and see them from various angles. The app also projects text, on demand, that highlights certain points of interest for him.

But wait—what if he wants to know even more about Andromeda than what's being projected in front of him? Well, that's where things *really* get interesting. Because the ARKit and the apps that it enables are a part of his iPhone or iPad, as opposed to a large, uncomfortable headset he has to wear, this means that everything that his phone can do could also interact with his solar system app. So if he has a question, all he would have to do is ask Siri, and he'll get his answer in seconds. And just in case all of that is not exciting enough for education enthusiasts to think about, remember this is all done via mobile, meaning learners can do all of these same things wherever they are. They are unbound by both time (apps are available 24/7) and location (mobile allowing us to be quite, well, *mobile*).

That should shed some light on why I'm so excited about the potential of AR to become one of the most transformative educational technologies to ever exist. Take just a moment to imagine the possibilities of combining AR with things like 3D printing, artificial intelligence, adaptive learning, wearables, the Internet of Things, robotics, GPS, big data, biometrics, social media, on-demand, livestreaming, crowdsourcing, cocreation, and the sharing economy. I get excited just thinking about how any one of these can work with AR to improve learning, and all of this amazing technology is already here. That's right, everything described about AR so far is either possible now or will be very soon. The technology itself is ready; someone just needs to get on the ball and make that cool solar system app!

Looking a bit further ahead at the future of AR, the prospects of possibility become even more intriguing. Over the course of the next year or two, teachers (and parents) will be able to download mobile apps containing interactive AR content on virtually *any* topic, as apps that support user-generated content allow for even the most tech-challenged of us to add and share valuable content with learning communities around the world. If nothing that already exists fits a teacher or parent's need, then they will be able to create, and easily test, their own dynamic AR content and adjust its complexity to fit the level of individual students. Developments, like the ARKit, are turning augmented reality into a platform, and where platforms exist, ecosystems are never far behind.

THE MAGIC OF HOLOGRAMS

While I'm not a fan of making long-term predictions about the rise and popularity of technologies, I'll play along for just a moment and share with you just a bit of what industry experts foresee. And from what I'm hearing, we're only about five years away from these becoming more of a reality too: *holograms*. If this type of AR comes to fruition on a large-enough scale, we won't even need to look at your phone's screen to see holographic images; they would just appear in full 3D right there in front of us.

As graphics continue to improve, holograms will begin producing images in photographic quality and, one day, be able to render it in a 4D environment (another emerging technology), where other senses, like smell, sound, taste, and touch, will also play a role. Instead of reading about dinosaurs, imagine learning about them through a full-scale holographic projection of a *T. rex* that can be seen, felt, heard, and even smelled, as if he were right there in the school with you. At museums, statues will be able to come to life, relay their stories, and use AR and AI to conduct open question-and-answer sessions. Learners will be able to physically interact with AR projections, moving them around just as they would material things.

One of my favorite promotional videos in recent years has been one created by the augmented reality start-up, Magic Leap. Founded in 2010 in Plantation, Florida, by Rony Abovitz, Magic Leap seemingly came out of nowhere with what appeared to be some of the most advanced mixed-reality technology anyone had ever seen. It wasn't long before word of mouth started to spread about what they were up to and all sorts of wild rumors circulated. Abovitz seemed to relish Magic Leap playing the role of "The World's Most Secretive Startup," as a 2016 *Wired* magazine article had dubbed them.[84] While very few people had actually seen Magic Leap's technology themselves, the buzz around it grew so big that it was able to raise over $1 billion of funding, including from some of the biggest names in venture capital, such as Google and Alibaba. In 2016 *Forbes* valued Magic Leap at $4.5 billion. Not bad for a start-up that has yet to release a single product!

The thing that really took Magic Leap to the next level in everyone eyes, though, was a simple, two-minute demo video that was set as their website's home page and ran in a continuous loop for anyone who visited. The video loop opened by showing a high school gymnasium filled with students, sitting on bleachers, staring out at the empty gym floor. Then, suddenly, a life-size whale comes crashing up through the gym floor, jumping high into the air, right in front of the students who stare up at it in disbelief, clapping and screaming, "Whoa! Ooh! Ahh!" Crystal-clear water appears to splash all over the gym, soaking the entire gym floor as the whale crashes back down into it and completely disappears. Seconds later all of that water vanishes too.

"Whoa!" is right! This amazing video purportedly showed that the future of AR and holograms was already here; it's just that everyone else in the world didn't realize it yet! Unfortunately, while some of the other cool but more realistic video clips in the loop were real, the holographic whale splashing the kids was simply a promotional gimmick. But I take the time to mention this in detail because I believe strongly that the life-sized, virtual whale in that gym, splashing those kids with virtual water, *really is the future of learning*. I foresee that as being exactly how students will be able to learn at some point in the future, through AR. As for the video itself, I believe magic can still be worth watching, even if we do know how it's done.

Anytime I think about holograms today, I can't help but think back to nearly thirty years ago, when my son, Kris, was in the eighth grade. He had a science project to do, and the topic could be anything of interest to him. Kris picked holograms, which were not very well known back then. But he thought they were the coolest thing ever, so I took him to the MIT Media Lab, and Kris got to meet and talk to some of the hologram researchers. He was so excited! "Holograms are the future, Dad," he said on the way back. I barely knew what they were, so I just chuckled and said, "Okay." This is just another example of how digital natives (even twelve-year-olds) are always one step ahead of us when it comes to technology!

CHANGE

In times of drastic change,
it is the learners who inherit the future
while the learned find themselves equipped
to live in a world that no longer exists.
—ERIC HOFFER

A few years ago, I asked a student in Australia to describe the education environment in his country. He said it was the Qantas theory of education. I said, "Do you mean quantum theory?" "No," he said. "Qantas, the airline. They make me turn off all my digital devices, strap myself in for the duration of the journey, and leave me hoping the pilot takes me where I want to go. I have to wait until we land before I can get my digital life back." It was an insightful way of saying school had not caught up with the digital world. Unfortunately, this is still the reality. The challenge for us all is to do something about it.

I believe it's time we stopped trying to repair and replace education and start rewiring it. This means moving with intent away from the old design that is holding us back from being able to effectively meet the needs of our digital natives. It means turning to psychology before technology and believing that all kids have the potential to succeed, so long as they have the proper motivation. It means focusing not on passive education, but on active learning, and ensuring that students have ideal learning spaces where various challenges, like those found in the *CBL* framework, can engage them on a regular basis. It means giving all students the *access* and opportunities needed to prepare for life in the twenty-first century, things like learning to build things by hand and in code. It means that we must rethink teaching and provide ongoing professional development so that teachers become facilitators of learning, rather than conveyers of information. Finally, it means raising our expectations for technology, and using it in transformative ways, so that it can unlock every student's potential and set in motion the future of education that they deserve. The question is, how? What can we actually *do* about it?[85]

It's parents who are in the best position to stand up to leadership at all levels, but the most vocal parents are also the ones whose children tend to be in great schools already. It's easy to assume that if your own kids are getting a good education, then there isn't much of a problem at all. These parents are also the ones most likely to have done well in the current educational system themselves. "All this talk about how bad public education is and how much it needs reforming is nonsense," a parent once scolded me. "It's the same system I went through and I'm fine. The system is good enough!" It's things like this out-of-touch mentality that is causing teachers to continue to struggle to meet student needs, and they're why American education has not changed much in over a century. Never mind that this parent's ideas are just plain wrong; while the system may be the same as it used to be, the *world* is not, and the old educational model is far from being "good enough" to prepare our kids for it.

A CALL TO ACTION

The Pony Express was a carrier service established in 1860 to transport mail across the Great Plains and over the Rocky Mountains, both to and from California. Doing this, of course, meant riding through "Indian country," which was not exactly the safest place to travel back then. The ad for riders at the time announced: "Wanted: Young, skinny, wiry fellows not over eighteen. Must be expert riders and willing to risk death daily. Orphans preferred." The heroic Pony Express riders inspired a piece of artwork that depicted a young man waving to workman erecting poles and stringing wires for a telegraph system. He was seeing the future, a much faster, cheaper, and safer way of delivering messages. This was a transformative technology that put an end to the dangerous Pony Express service. I often ask my audience of educators, "Are we the education equivalent of the Pony Express, or are we laying the foundation for a new learning environment?"

Today, we must consider if we're willing to continue sitting back and accepting the flaws of our Pony Express–like education system, which is failing far too many of our students, when there are ways of doing things better. Just like the telegraph system of yesterday, transformative technologies that exist *right now* have the ability to rewire education, and ultimately, the way we design our classrooms today will define our society tomorrow.

As more people become aware of the challenges within our education system and the opportunities available to face them, I believe that real change is possible. It's my hope that you will consider this book as a *call to action*, if you will, and take the initiative to reach out to others, start conversations, and demand that our educational and political leaders begin taking advantage of current research, teaching methods, and technologies that can make a difference. Real change does not often move from the top down, where leaders come up with silver bullet ideas that they then sell to the public and magically change the world. No, significant change, even entire *movements*, begin from the bottom, with people like you, through grassroots calls to action, that work their way up to those in power, pressuring them to reject the status quo and change things for the better.

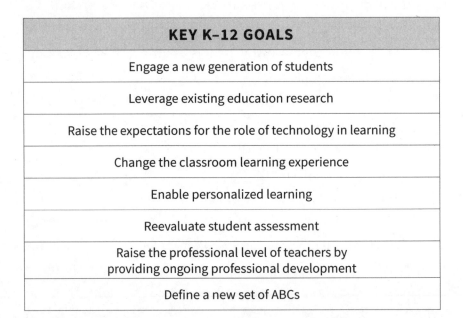

KEY K–12 GOALS
Engage a new generation of students
Leverage existing education research
Raise the expectations for the role of technology in learning
Change the classroom learning experience
Enable personalized learning
Reevaluate student assessment
Raise the professional level of teachers by providing ongoing professional development
Define a new set of ABCs

As a child, anytime I ever complained about anything, no matter how big or small it was, my father would just stare at me with a blank face for a moment before finally saying, "So . . . what are *you* going to do about it?" It was a challenge that essentially told me to "shut up or put up": either try to actually *do* something about the things I don't like, or stop complaining. I now respond to anyone who complains that we aren't doing a good enough job reaching and teaching kids with the same challenge: What are *you* going to do about it? Luckily, especially today, there is plenty you can do.

By using freely available online resources such as petition websites like Change.org and social media platforms like Twitter and Facebook, you, as an *individual*, have the power to initiate real change, whether it's at the federal, state, local, or school level. The explosion of the internet and social networking have empowered regular individuals (once referred as the "commoners") today more than any other time throughout history. All it takes is a single parent, teacher, or activist to create an online petition, or share their thoughts with a tweet or Facebook or Instagram post, and you have the potential to start a chain of events that leads to transformative change. But it starts with you. As Mahatma Gandhi said, "Be the change that you wish to see in the world." I urge you to be a part of a growing movement to rewire education, join the conversation, and be the change *you* wish to see.

ACKNOWLEDGMENTS

Nothing worth doing has ever been done alone, including this book. We would like to take this time to personally thank the following people for the support of and/or influence that they have had on *Rewiring Education*. In one way or another you have each played a key role in shaping this book and have made a real difference in the lives of one or both of its authors.

Abdul Chohan, Adam Savage, Adrienne Lang, Alexandre Robert-Tissot, Ali Partovi, Alicia Kania, Alfonso Roma Jr., Andy Peterson, Angela Duckworth, Angelica Towne, Angus King, Anita Cota, Ben Orlin, Bill Gates, Bill Gladstone, Bill Simon, Bill Sutherland, Chris Dede, Clark Gilbert, Clayton Christensen, Dale Dougherty, Darryl Adams, David Thornburg, David Vinca, Diane Tavenner, E. O. Wilson, Elon Musk, Eric Mazur, Erica Harmon, Georgina Lopez Guerra, Glenn Yeffeth, Gordon Shukwit, Hadi Partovi, Heather Butterfield, Howard Gardner, James Fraleigh, James E. Ryan, Jamie Hyneman, Jane Anderson, Janet Wozniak, Jason Ediger, Jena Collins, Jennifer Canzoneri, Jessika Rieck, Jodie Deinhammer, John Medina, Jon Couch, Jon Star, Jordan Couch, Karen Brennan, Karen Cator, Karim Lakhani, Keith Collar, Ken Robinson, Kris Bazan, Kris Couch, Larry Reiff,

Laurene Powell Jobs, Leah Wilson, Lindsay Marshall, Lylee Kazem, Lyn Stanfield, Malcolm Gladwell, Mallory Dwinal, Marc Prensky, Marco Torres, Mark Edwards, Mark Nichols, Mark Zuckerberg, Mary Lou Couch, Matt Cooper, Meredith Liu, Michael Clifford, Michael Horn, Miles Towne, Mindy Kornhaber, Noel Trainor, Noemi Trainor, Priscilla Chan, Radhika "Radical" Lee, Reed Hastings, Rita Prescott, Ritz Sherman, Ruben Puentedura, Rush Limbaugh, Salman Khan, Sarah Avinger, Simon Sinek, Stephanie Hamilton, Steve Jobs, Steve Wozniak, Sugata Mitra, Tara Gallagher, Tiffany Couch, Tim Cook, Todd Rose, Tom Sudberry, Tom Whitney, Tony Wagner, Wendy Wong, and William Rankin.

Thank you all,

JOHN AND JASON

ENDNOTES

INTRODUCTION

[1] Wilson, S.S. "Bicycle Technology." *Scientific American* 228, no. 3 (1973): 81–91.

CHAPTER 1: REWIRING

[2] Prensky, Marc. "Digital Natives, Digital Immigrants Part 1." *On the Horizon* 9, no. 5 (2001): 1–6.

[3] Englander, Elizabeth. "Research Findings: MARC 2011 Survey Grades 3–12." *MARC Research Reports*, 2011. http://vc.bridgew.edu/marc_reports/2

[4] Gardner, Howard. *The App Generation: How Today's Youth Navigate Identity, Intimacy, and Imagination in a Digital World*. New Haven, CT: Yale University Press, 2014.

[5] Dewey, John. *Experience and Education*. New York: Macmillan, 1938.

[6] Lynch, Tom. "Not a Lightbulb: Uncovering Thomas Edison's Greatest Lesson on Education." *Medium*, June 9, 2016. https://medium.com/@tomliamlynch/not-a-lightbulb-c00904d79506

CHAPTER 2: DESIGN

[7] Christensen, Clayton M., Michael B. Horn, and Curtis W. Johnson. *Disrupting Class: How Disruptive Innovation Will Change the Way the World Learns*. New York: McGraw-Hill, 2008.

[8] Rose, Todd. *The End of Average: How We Succeed in a World That Values Sameness*. San Francisco: HarperOne, 2016.

[9] Ibid.

CHAPTER 3: POTENTIAL

[10] Sweeney, Sarah. "A Wild Rose in Bloom." *Harvard Gazette*, March 15, 2013. https://news.harvard.edu/gazette/story/2013/03/a-wild-rose-in-bloom

[11] Rose, Todd. *Square Peg: My Story and What It Means for Raising Innovators, Visionaries, and Out-of-the-Box Thinkers.* New York: Hyperion, 2013.

[12] Steinberg, Douglas. "Determining Nature vs. Nurture." *Scientific American Mind* 17, no. 5 (2006): 12–14.

[13] Shenk, David. *The Genius in All of Us: New Insights into Genetics, Talent, and IQ.* New York: Anchor Books, 2011.

CHAPTER 4: MOTIVATION

[14] Stipek, Deborah J., and Kathy Seal. *Motivated Minds: Raising Children to Love Learning.* New York: H. Holt and Co., 2001.

[15] Deemer, Sandra. *Reflections on How Educators Use Motivational Theories in Educational Psychology.* Dubuque, IA: Kendall Hunt Publishing Company, 2012.

[16] Deci, Edward L., and Richard M. Ryan. *Intrinsic Motivation and Self-Determination in Human Behavior.* New York: Plenum Press, 1985.

[17] Stipek, Deborah J. *Motivation to Learn: Integrating Theory and Practice.* Boston: Allyn and Bacon, 2002.

[18] Geis, George L. "Student Participation in Instruction: Student Choice." *The Journal of Higher Education* 47, no. 3 (1976): 249–273.

[19] Gladwell, Malcolm. *Outliers: The Story of Success.* New York: Back Bay Books, 2013.

[20] Duckworth, Angela. *Grit: The Power of Passion and Perseverance.* New York: Scribner, 2016.

CHAPTER 5: LEARNING

[21] Medina, John. *Brain Rules: 12 Principles for Surviving and Thriving at Work, Home, and School.* Edmonds, WA: Pear Press, 2008.

[22] Cimons, Marlene. "How the Brain Learns." *U.S. News & World Report*, February 24, 2012. https://www.usnews.com/science/articles/2012/02/24/how-the-brain-learns

[23] Fleming, Neil D. "The VARK Modalities." *VARK: A Guide to Learning Styles.* http://vark-learn.com/introduction-to-vark/the-vark-modalities

[24] Gardner, Howard. *Frames of Mind: The Theory of Multiple Intelligences.* New York: Basic Books, 2011.

[25] Hestenes, David. "Wherefore a Science of Teaching?" *The Physics Teacher* 17 (1979): 235–242.

[26] Lambert, Craig. "Twilight of the Lecture." *Harvard Magazine*, Mar–Apr 2012. https://harvardmagazine.com/2012/03/twilight-of-the-lecture

CHAPTER 6: SPACES

[27] Thornburg, David D. "Campfires in Cyberspace: Primordial Metaphors for Learning in the 21st Century." *Ed at a Distance* 15, no. 6 (2001).

[28] United States Department of Education. *What Works: Research About Teaching and Learning*. Washington, DC: U.S. Government Printing Office, 1987.

[29] Lai, Emily R. "Metacognition: A Literature Review." *Research Report*, April 2011. https://images.pearsonassessments.com/images/tmrs/Metacognition_Literature_Review_Final.pdf

CHAPTER 7: CHALLENGES

[30] Morrow, Daniel. "Excerpts from an Oral History Interview with Steve Jobs." *Smithsonian Institution Oral and Video Histories*, April 20, 1995. http://americanhistory.si.edu/comphist/sj1.html

[31] Watters, Audrey. "How Steve Jobs Brought the Apple II to the Classroom." Hackeducation, February 25, 2015. http://hackeducation.com/2015/02/25/kids-cant-wait-apple

[32] Dwyer, David. "Apple Classrooms of Tomorrow: What We've Learned." *Educational Leadership* 51, no. 7 (1994): 4–10.

[33] Ringstaff, Cathy, Keith Yocam, and Jean Marsh. "Integrating Technology into Classroom Instruction: An Assessment of the Impact of the ACOT Teacher Development Center Project." Apple. https://www.academia.edu/6858773/Integrating_Technology_into_Classroom_Instruction_An_Assessment_of_the_Impact_of_the_ACOT_Teacher_Development_Center_Project_Research_APPLE_CLASSROOMS_OF_TOMORROW_Authors_Jean_Marsh_Independent_Educational_Researcher

[34] Sandholtz, Judith, et al. "Teaching in High-Tech Environments: Classroom Management Revisited, First–Fourth Year Findings." Apple. https://www.scribd.com/document/4101317/9541

[35] "Apple Classrooms of Tomorrow, Today: Learning in the 21st Century: Background Information." April 2008. http://cbl.digitalpromise.org/wp-content/uploads/sites/7/2017/07/ACOT2_Background.pdf

CHAPTER 8: CBL

[36] "A Heart Anatomy Lesson with a Digital Pulse." Apple. https://www. apple.com/education/teach-with-ipad/classroom/heart-anatomy

[37] Nichols, Mark, Karen Cator, and Marco Torres. "Challenge Based Learning User Guide." Redwood City, CA: *Digital Promise*, 2016. http:// cbl.digitalpromise.org/wp-content/uploads/sites/7/2016/10/CBL_ Guide2016.pdf

[38] Johnson, Laurence F., Rachel S. Smith, J. Troy Smythe, and Rachel K. Varon. "CBL: An Approach for Our Time." Austin, Texas: New Media Consortium. https://www.nmc.org/sites/default/files/pubs/1317320235/ Challenge-Based-Learning.pdf

[39] "Toolkit." *Digital Promise*. http://cbl.digitalpromise.org/toolkit

CHAPTER 9: ACCESS

[40] Moodian, Margaret. "The Rock and Roll Superintendent Making a Difference." *Huffington Post*, March 30, 2016. https://www.huffingtonpost. com/margaret-moodian/the-rock-and-roll-superin_b_9570332.html

[41] Simonite, Tom. "Billions of People Could Get Online for the First Time Thanks to Helium Balloons That Google Will Soon Send Over Many Places Cell Towers Don't Reach." *MIT Technology Review*, 2014. https:// www.technologyreview.com/s/534986/project-loon

[42] "ConnectED." Apple. https://www.apple.com/connectED/

[43] "ConnectED Initiative." Obama White House Archives. https:// obamawhitehouse.archives.gov/issues/education/k-12/connected

[44] Fowler, Geoffrey A. "An Early Report Card on MOOCs." *Wall Street Journal*, October 8, 2013. https://www.wsj.com/articles/an-early-report-card-on-massive-open-online-courses-1381266504

[45] Horn, Michael B., Heather Staker, and Clayton M. Christensen. *Blended: Using Disruptive Innovation to Improve Schools*. San Francisco: Jossey-Bass, 2015.

[46] Khan, Salman. *The One World Schoolhouse: A New Approach to Teaching and Learning*. London: Hodder & Stoughton, 2012.

[47] "Khan Lab School Reinvents American Classroom." *CBS This Morning*, November 20, 2015. https://www.cbsnews.com/videos/khan-lab-school-reinvents-american-classroom

[48] Wong, Queenie. "Exclusive: How Zuckerberg and Chan's New Private School Mixes Health Care and Education." *Mercury News*, December 23, 2016. http://www.mercurynews.com/2016/12/23/exclusive-how-zuckerberg-chan-primary-school-works

CHAPTER 10: BUILD

[49] Owlet Learning. "Elon Musk on his school, Ad Astra." YouTube video, May 27, 2016. https://www.youtube.com/watch?v=7X0BG9JzoXM

[50] McCracken, Harry. "Maker Faire Founder Dale Dougherty on the Past, Present, and Online Future of the Maker Movement." *Fast Company*, April 29, 2015. https://www.fastcompany.com/3045505/maker-faire-founder-dale-dougherty-on-the-past-present-and-online-future-of-the-maker-moveme

[51] Galvin, Gaby. "Makers Movement Changes the Landscape." *U.S. News & World Report*, May 22, 2017. https://www.usnews.com/news/maker-cities/articles/2017-05-23/makers-movement-changes-the-educational-landscape

[52] Blake, Vikki. "Minecraft Has 55 Million Monthly Players, 122 Million Sales." *IGN*, February 27, 2017. http://www.ign.com/articles/2017/02/27/minecraft-has-55-million-monthly-players-122-million-sales

CHAPTER 11: CODE

[53] TedTalk. "A 12-Year-Old App Developer." YouTube video, October 2011. https://www.ted.com/talks/thomas_suarez_a_12_year_old_app_developer

[54] Wing, Jeannette M. "Computational Thinking." *Communications of the ACM* 49, no. 3 (March 2016). https://www.cs.cmu.edu/~15110-s13/Wing06-ct.pdf

[55] Alba, Davey. "Tech Workers Are Way Picky About the Cities They'll Work In." *Wired*, September 15, 2015. https://www.wired.com/2015/09/tech-workers-way-picky-cities-theyll-work

[56] Greenberger, Martin. *Computers and the World of the Future*. Cambridge, Mass.: MIT Press, 1969.

[57] "About ScratchJr." *ScratchJr*. https://www.scratchjr.org/about/info

[58] "Swift Playgrounds." Apple. https://www.apple.com/swift/playgrounds

[59] Papert, Seymour. *Mindstorms: Children, Computers, and Powerful Ideas*. New York: Basic Books, 2005.

[60] Adam, Anna, and Helen Mowers. "Should Coding Be the 'New Foreign Language' Requirement?" *Edutopia*, October 30, 2013. https://www.edutopia.org/blog/coding-new-foreign-language-requirement-helen-mowers

[61] Zinth, Jennifer. "Computer Science in High School Graduation Requirements." *Education Commission of the States*, September 2006. http://files.eric.ed.gov/fulltext/ED556465.pdf

CHAPTER 12: TEACHING

[62] Wozniak, Steve, with Gina Smith. *I, Woz: Computer Geek to Cult Icon: How I Invented the Personal Computer, Co-Founded Apple, and Had Fun Doing It.* New York: W. W. Norton & Company, 2006.

[63] "About." *Woz U.* https://woz-u.com/about

[64] Juergens, Gary. "Steve Wozniak on Education." YouTube video, November 4, 2016. https://www.youtube.com/watch?v=LchNLvjBfBo

[65] Rich, Motoko. "Teacher Shortages Spur a Nationwide Hiring Scramble (Credentials Optional)." *New York Times*, August 9, 2015. https://www.nytimes.com/2015/08/10/us/teacher-shortages-spur-a-nationwide-hiring-scramble-credentials-optional.html

[66] Towne, J.W., and Rita J. Prescott. *Conversations with America's Best Teachers: Teacher of the Year Award Winners Give Practical Advice for the Classroom and Beyond.* Los Angeles, CA: Inkster Pub, 2009.

[67] "A Modern Look at Romeo & Juliet." Apple. https://www.apple.com/education/teach-with-ipad/classroom/romeo-and-juliet

CHAPTER 13: TECHNOLOGY

[68] Koehler, Matthew J., et al. "What Is Technological Pedagogical Content Knowledge (TPACK)?" *The Journal of Education* 193, no. 3 (2013): 13–19.

[69] Puentedura, Ruben. "SAMR: Beyond the Basics." Hippasus, April 26, 2013. http://www.hippasus.com/rrpweblog/archives/2013/04/26/SAMRBeyondTheBasics.pdf

[70] "Apple Distinguished Educators." Apple. https://www.apple.com/education/apple-distinguished-educator

[71] "Apple in Education Profiles." Apple. https://www.apple.com/education/real-stories/essa

[72] Beijing Bluefocus E-Commerce Col, Ltd., et. al. "A Case Study—The Impact of VR on Academic Performance." *UploadVR*, November 25, 2016. https://uploadvr.com/chinese-vr-education-study

[73] Coughlan, Sean. "Computers 'Do Not Improve' Pupil Results, Says OECD." *BBC News*, September 15, 2015. http://www.bbc.com/news/business-34174796

[74] The Hechinger Report. "Study: Computer Use in School Doesn't Help Test Scores." *U.S. News & World Report*, September 22, 2015. https://www.usnews.com/news/articles/2015/09/22/study-students-who-use-computers-often-in-school-have-lower-test-scores

[75] Davis, Owen. "What International Education Rankings Don't Measure." *The Nation*, December 5, 2013. https://www.thenation.com/article/what-international-education-rankings-dont-measure

[76] "Students, Computers and Learning: Making the Connection." OECD, September 15, 2015. http://www.oecd.org/publications/students-computers-and-learning-9789264239555-en.htm

CHAPTER 14: TRANSFORMATIVE!

[77] Nordrum, Amy. "Popular Internet of Things Forecast of 50 Billion Devices by 2020 is Outdated." *IEEE Spectrum*, August 18, 2016. https://spectrum.ieee.org/tech-talk/telecom/internet/popular-internet-of-things-forecast-of-50-billion-devices-by-2020-is-outdated

[78] Mac Learning. "Apple Knowledge Navigator Video (1987)." Youtube video, March 4, 2012. https://www.youtube.com/watch?v=umJsITGzXd0

[79] Desjardins, Jeff. "Timeline: The March to a Billion Users." *Visual Capitalist*, February 26, 2016. http://www.visualcapitalist.com/timeline-the-march-to-a-billion-users

CHAPTER 15: FUTURISTIC

[80] Bacca, Jorge, et al. "Augmented Reality Trends in Education: A Systematic Review of Research and Applications." *Journal of Educational Technology & Society* 17, no. 4 (2014): 133–149.

[81] "Varmond School Home Page." Varmond School. http://varmondschool.edu.mx

[82] "PBS KIDS Launches Its First Educational Augmented Reality App." *PBS*, November 14, 2011. http://www.pbs.org/about/blogs/news/pbs-kids-launches-its-first-educational-augmented-reality-app

[83] "Introducing ARKit." Apple. https://developer.apple.com/arkit

[84] Kelly, Kevin. "The Untold Story of Magic Leap, the World's Most Secretive Startup." *Wired*, May 2016. https://www.wired.com/2016/04/magic-leap-vr

CHANGE

[85] Locatelli, Alice. "Sparking the Future of Education." *eSpark Learning*, December 2014. https://www.esparklearning.com/future-of-education-white-paper

INDEX

ABOUT
THE AUTHORS

JOHN D. COUCH is Vice President of Education at Apple. A former UC Berkeley graduate student, HP engineer and manager, and Cal State University lecturer, John was recruited by Steve Jobs in 1978, becoming Apple's 54th employee. He left in 1984 and spent ten years using innovative technology to transform a struggling K–12 school  in San Diego, which is now a National Blue Ribbon School. At Jobs's request, John returned to Apple in 2002, tasked with bringing education into the digital age. He has been a vocal proponent of personalized learning and was Apple's representative to President Obama's National Education Technology Plan and ConnectEd initiative. In 2017, John funded the establishment of a new student learning research fellowship at Harvard University designed to support cutting-edge research for improving student learning and motivation.

JASON TOWNE is research fellow at Harvard University, where he focuses on motivation, learning, and technology. He is the author of the critically acclaimed book *Conversations with America's Best Teachers*, in which he interviewed eighteen National Teacher of the Year Award winners and nominees about what they do differently. Towne received his BS degree in Public Policy and graduated magna cum laude from the University of Southern California in 2009. In 2015, he earned his Master's degree in Education from Harvard, where he studied motivational psychology and education technology, codirected the prestigious Harvard Innovative Ventures in Education (HIVE) program, and won the coveted Harvard Leadership in Education Award. Prior to Harvard, he was an executive for the YMCA overseeing youth development.